Wiley CPAexcel® Exam Review

PRACTICE QUESTIONS

2019

AUDITING AND ATTESTATION

Wiley CPAexcel® Exam Review

PRACTICE QUESTIONS

2019

AUDITING AND ATTESTATION

Donald E. Tidrick, Ph.D., CPA, CMA, CIA
Robert A. Prentice, J.D.

Wiley Efficient Learning™

ISBN 978-1-119-53441-9
ISBN 978-1-119-53443-3 (ebk); ISBN 978-1-119-53444-0 (ebk)

Printed in the United States of America.

V10004797_092818

Table of Contents

Multiple Choice Questions

Ethics, Professional Responsibilities, and General Principles

AICPA Code of Professional Conduct

Introduction and Preface

aq.intro.pref.001_17

1. Jeffrey has two jobs. In the mornings, he works for a firm in public practice. In the afternoon, he has a job working as a member in business. If he finds himself in a position where standards seem to be inconsistent, he should choose:

    A. Those applying to MIPPs.
    B. Those applying to MIBs.
    C. Those applying to OMs.
    D. None of the above; no standards would apply in that setting.

AICPA.141052AUD-SIM

2. Which of the following is true regarding the Principles of Professional Conduct?

    A. To live up to the Code of Professional Conduct, members may have to work hard, but they do not have to sacrifice their own best interests.
    B. Members must not only be competent in the provision of professional services; they must also cooperate with other members to improve the art of accounting.
    C. Due care in the audit area is satisfied if a member knows generally accepted accounting principles and generally accepted accounting standards inside and out.
    D. Because the Code of Professional Conduct does not expressly prohibit a member from moonlighting as a circus trapese performer, a member could perform at a local bar as "Sam the Flying CPA."

AICPA.940502REG-BL

3. Which of the following statements best explains why the CPA profession has found it essential to promulgate ethical standards and to establish means for ensuring their observance?

    A. A distinguishing mark of a profession is its acceptance of responsibility to the public.
    B. A requirement for a profession is to establish ethical standards that stress primary responsibility to clients and colleagues.

    C. Ethical standards that emphasize excellence in performance over material rewards establish a reputation for competence and character.
    D. Vigorous enforcement of an established code of ethics is the best way to prevent unscrupulous acts.

Members in Public Practice

MIPPs Introduction and Conceptual Framework

AICPA.141015AUD-SIM

4. Which of the following is **not** a key concept in the code's Conceptual Framework?

    A. Threats.
    B. Safeguards.
    C. Unusual danger.
    D. Acceptable level.

AICPA.141017AUD-SIM

5. Which of the following are sources of safeguards that might reduce a threat of noncompliance with the code to an acceptable level?

    A. Safeguards created by the profession.
    B. Safeguards implemented by the client.
    C. Safeguards implemented by the firm.
    D. All three choices provided.

MIPPs Nonindependence Rules

Conflicts of Interest, Directorships, and Gifts

aq.conflict.interest.003_17

6. In which of the following situations would member Taka **not** be in a conflict of interest?

    A. Taka is giving financial advice to both the buyer and the seller in a commercial real estate deal.
    B. Taka is giving financial advice to both the husband and the wife in a messy divorce proceeding.

C. Taka is providing financial advice to ABC Co. as it readies a bid to buy a large office building knowing that Taka's own firm is simultaneously planning to submit a bid itself.

D. Taka's firm is bidding to buy a tract of real estate that is owned by a company that was a tax client of the firm more than 10 years before.

AICPA.141010AUD-SIM

7. Which of the following would constitute a conflict of interest that poses a threat to objectivity?

A. The ABC Accounting Firm is hired by Bozo Co. to provide litigation support services in its lawsuit against Bebop Corp., which is a tax client of ABC.

B. Quan suggests that his tax client Linda invest her tax refund in Blitz Corporation without disclosing that he owns a large stake in Blitz.

C. Tibble recommends that his tax client Borton hire a financial planner named Tilden without disclosing that Tilden has agreed in exchange to refer all his clients who need an accountant to Tibble.

D. All three of the choices provided.

AICPA.141011AUD-SIM

8. If Maria has ABC for an attest client, from which of the following should she be wary of accepting gifts that might threaten her objectivity?

A. ABC.

B. ABC's officers.

C. ABC's major (> 10%) shareholders.

D. All three of the choices provided.

Reporting Income and Subordination of Judgment

AICPA.080940REG-1B

9. Son is a junior auditor from ABC Accounting Firm's audit team at client Mammoth Corporation. Son believes that Mammoth's CFO is mischaracterizing some important transactions. Mammoth's CFO is adamant about the treatment of these transactions. After doing substantial research and consulting with his supervisor, who supports Mammoth's view, Son believes that following Mammoth's preferred treatment would produce inaccurate financial statements that would materially mislead investors. What should Son do at this stage?

A. Make his concerns known to higher levels of his firm and/or the client.

B. Resign from ABC.

C. Inform the SEC.

D. Make his concerns known to higher levels of his firm and/or the client, resign from ABC, and inform the SEC.

AICPA.141008AUD-SIM

10. Which of the following is (are) true regarding auditors who disagree with their supervisors regarding the proper handling of an important transaction for financial statement purposes?

A. The auditor should always defer to the superior who, after all, has superior experience.

B. The auditor should always quit on the spot rather than compromise her integrity.

C. The auditor should always discuss the matter with the superior if it appears that there is a significant threat that the financial statements will be inaccurate.

D. All of the choices provided.

AICPA.141009AUD-SIM

11. Which of the following would violate the Code of Professional Conduct?

A. Auditor Sam instructed an underling, Todd, to make a materially false entry in an audit client's financial statements.

B. Sam's superior, Sarah, knew what Sam had done and did not correct it.

C. Sarah signed the firm's audit report, knowing that the error had not been corrected.

D. All of the choices provided.

Advocacy, Third-Party Service Providers (TSPs), General Standards, and Accounting Principles

AICPA.080942REG-1B

12. Sally has her own small accounting firm. Due to some personal connections with a top officer of Mediumsize Corporation, Sally landed an interview with Mediumsize as a potential tax client. Mediumsize has some complicated tax issues of a type that Sally has not handled before. Which of the following is true?

   I.   Because Sally has not handled these complicated issues before, she cannot take this engagement.
   II. Sally can take this engagement if she believes in good faith that she can research these tax issues and handle them competently.
   III. Sally can take this engagement if she believes in good faith that she can consult with experts in the area and thereby handle these tax issues competently.

   A. I only.
   B. II only.
   C. I and II.
   D. II and III.

AICPA.080943REG-1B

13. Dena prepared personal income tax returns for 100 clients last year. Two of her clients have come to her with valid complaints about errors she made in their returns, causing them to pay more than they should have in taxes. Which of the following is true?

   I. Dena's CPA license should be revoked, because she obviously cannot exercise due professional care.
   II. While it is certainly possible that Dena has acted without due professional care in these two instances, the AICPA does not demand perfection.

   A. I only.
   B. II only.
   C. I and II.
   D. Neither I nor II.

AICPA.080951REG-1B

14. Dain would violate the Code of Professional Responsibility if, during an audit, he:

   I. Stated that he was not aware of any material modifications that should be made to the audited financial statements in order for them to be in conformity with GAAP if he was, in fact, aware of needed material modifications.
   II. Stated that he was not aware of any material modifications that should be made to the audited financial statements in order for them to be in conformity with GAAP if he was aware of immaterial modifications that would be desirable.

   A. I only.
   B. II only.
   C. I and II.
   D. Neither I nor I.

AICPA.141013AUD-SIM

15. Which of the following is true?

   A. Clients have the right to veto any outsourcing by a CPA firm.
   B. Clients must be informed in writing before any professional services are outsourced.
   C. If the client objects to outsourcing of professional services, then the member should either not outsource the work or decline to provide the service altogether.
   D. All three choices provided.

AICPA.141014AUD-SIM

16. Members may properly:

   I. Advocate on behalf of audit clients.
   II. Advocate on behalf of tax clients.

   A. I only.
   B. II only.
   C. I and II.
   D. Neither I nor II.

Discreditable Acts

AICPA.080923REG-1B

17. Which of the following actions by a CPA most likely constitutes an act discreditable to the profession?

   A. Discriminating on the basis of race in employment.
   B. Negligently making false journal entries.
   C. Failing to pay one's own personal income tax.
   D. All three of the choices provided.

AICPA.080955REG-1B

18. Which of the following actions by a CPA *most likely* does not constitute an act discreditable to the profession?

    A. Sexually harassing an employee.
    B. Providing for a right of contribution from the client in an audit engagement letter.
    C. Providing for a right of indemnification from the client in an audit engagement letter.
    D. All of the above.

AICPA.090603REG-I-B

19. Spinner, CPA, had audited Lasco Corp.'s financial statements for the past several years. Prior to the current year's engagement, a disagreement arose that caused Lasco to change auditing firms. Lasco has demanded that Spinner provide Lasco with Spinner's audit documentation so that Lasco may show them to prospective auditors to help them prepare their bids for Lasco's audit engagement. Spinner refused and Lasco commenced litigation. Under the ethical standards of the profession, will Spinner be successful in refusing to turn over the documentation?

    A. Yes, because Spinner is the owner of the audit documentation.
    B. Yes, because Lasco is required to direct prospective auditors to contact Spinner to make arrangements to view the audit documentation in Spinner's office.
    C. No, because Lasco has a legitimate business reason for demanding that Spinner surrender the audit documentation.
    D. No, because it was Lasco's financial statements that were audited.

AICPA.111160AUD

20. According to the AICPA Code of Professional Conduct, which of the following actions by a CPA *most likely* involves an act discreditable to the profession?

    A. Refusing to provide the client with copies of the CPA's audit documentation.
    B. Auditing financial statements according to governmental standards despite the client's preferences.
    C. Accepting a commission from a nonattest function client.
    D. Retaining client records after the client demands their return.

AICPA.940501REG-BL

21. Which of the following actions by a CPA *most likely* violates the profession's ethical standards?

    A. Arranging with a financial institution to collect notes issued by a client in payment of fees due.
    B. Compiling the financial statements of a client that employed the CPA's spouse as a bookkeeper.
    C. Retaining client records after the client has demanded their return.
    D. Purchasing a segment of an insurance company's business that performs actuarial services for employee benefit plans.

Fees

AICPA.080961REG-1B

22. In which of the following scenarios has Ed, a CPA, **not** committed an ethical violation in relation to a tax client, Harriett, who asked Ed what she should do with a $12,000 tax refund she received from the IRS?

    A. Ed referred Harriett to investment adviser Sue, without disclosing to Harriett that Sue was Ed's sister-in-law.
    B. Ed referred Harriett to the investment advising firm of Stuart, Scott & Barney, without disclosing that he (Ed) was an unnamed partner in that firm.
    C. Ed recommended that Harriett purchase certain investment instruments from Mathwell Kilby & Co., without disclosing that Mathwell Kilby paid Ed a 5% commission on each transaction.
    D. Ed sold Harriett an investment instrument, disclosing that he was earning a 5% commission on the transaction.

AICPA.080963REG-1B

23. Tammy is looking to increase the revenue stream for her accounting firm. She is thinking of using commissions and referral fees to do so. Which of the following is true regarding commissions and referral fees?

    I. Neither is permitted when the client is an attest client.
    II. Both are permitted when the client is not an attest client, if they are properly disclosed.

    A. I only.
    B. II only.
    C. I and II.
    D. Neither I nor II.

AICPA.090604REG-I-B

24. Assuming appropriate disclosure is made, which of the following fee arrangements generally would be permitted under the ethical standards of the profession?

    A. A fee paid to the client's audit firm for recommending investment advisory services to the client.
    B. A fee paid to the client's tax accountant for recommending a computer system to the client.
    C. A contingent fee paid to the CPA for preparing the client's amended income tax return.
    D. A contingent fee paid to the CPA for reviewing the client's financial statements.

AICPA.120602AUD

25. According to the Code of Professional Conduct of the AICPA, for which type of service may a CPA receive a contingent fee?

    A. Performing an audit of a financial statement.
    B. Performing a review of a financial statement.
    C. Performing an examination of a prospective financial statement.
    D. Seeking a private letter ruling.

assess.AICPA.AUD.code.prof.con-0022

26. Considering only the provisions of the AICPA Code of Professional Conduct, which of the following services may a CPA perform for a commission or contingent fee?

    A. Preparation of an original income tax return.
    B. Representation of a nonattest client in an IRS examination.
    C. Preparation of an amended income tax return to claim a deduction that was inadvertently omitted on an originally filed return.
    D. Performance of consulting services for an audit client.

Advertising and Confidentiality

AICPA.060651REG

27. Page, CPA, has T Corp. and W Corp. as audit clients. T Corp. is a significant supplier of raw materials to W Corp. Page also prepares individual tax returns for Time, the owner of T Corp., and West, the owner of W Corp. When preparing West's return, Page finds information that raises going-concern issues with respect to W Corp.

    May Page disclose this information to Time?

    A. Yes, because Page has a fiduciary relationship with Time.
    B. Yes, because there is **no** accountant-client privilege between Page and West.

    C. No, because the information is confidential and may **not** be disclosed without West's consent.
    D. No, because the information should only be disclosed in Page's audit report on W Corp.'s financial statements.

AICPA.082100REG-I.B

28. Which of the following acts by a CPA is a violation of professional standards regarding the confidentiality of client information?

    A. Releasing financial information to a local bank with the approval of the client's mail clerk.
    B. Allowing a review of professional practice without client authorization.
    C. Responding to an enforceable subpoena.
    D. Faxing a tax return to a loan officer at the request of the client.

AICPA.090602REG-I-B

29. A CPA in public practice may not disclose confidential client information regarding auditing situations without the client's consent in response to which of the following situations?

    A. A review of the CPA's professional practice by a state CPA society.
    B. A letter to the client from the IRS.
    C. An inquiry from the professional ethics division of the AICPA.
    D. A court-ordered subpoena or summons.

AICPA.931110REG-BL

30. A CPA's audit documentation

    A. Need not be disclosed under a federal court subpoena.
    B. Must be disclosed under an IRS administrative subpoena.
    C. Must be disclosed to another accountant purchasing the CPA's practice even if the client hasn't given permission.
    D. Need not be disclosed to a state CPA society quality review team.

AICPA.941114REG-BL

31. Which of the following statements concerning an accountant's disclosure of confidential client data is generally correct?

    A. Disclosure may be made to any state agency without a subpoena.
    B. Disclosure may be made to any party on consent of the client.
    C. Disclosure may be made to comply with an IRS audit request.
    D. Disclosure may be made just for the heck of it.

Form of Organization and Names

AICPA.080964REG-1B

32. Maisy wishes to start her own accounting firm and wonders what restrictions there are on names of such firms. Which of the following is accurate?

   A. An accounting firm's name may not be misleading.
   B. An accounting firm's name may include the names of past owners.
   C. An accounting firm's name may (if not misleading) include a fictitious name.
   D. All three choices provided.

AICPA.080965REG-1B

33. Allen wishes to start his own audit firm. In which form may he practice, assuming the form is permitted in his state?

   A. Sole proprietorship.
   B. General partnership.
   C. LLP.
   D. All three answer choices provided.

AICPA.080966REG-1B

34. Which firms must have a majority of their financial interests owned by CPAs?

   I. Attest firms.
   II. Firms that identify themselves as "Members of the AICPA."

   A. I only.
   B. II only.
   C. I and II.
   D. Neither I nor II.

MIPPs Independence Rules

Introduction to MIPPs Independence Rules

aq.mipp.intro.001_17

35. The Mumbles Accounting Firm audits a privately-held transit company, Rapid Transit Dreamliners, Inc. (RTDI). Which of the following people would be a *covered member*?

   A. Dort, a tax accountant who has risen to become the CEO of Mumbles.
   B. Samples, a tax manager for Mumbles who provided 5 hours of tax advisory services to RTDI during the year under audit.
   C. Tingle, an auditor for Mumbles who formerly was on the RTDI audit team, but rotated off five years ago and has not had anything to do with RTDI since and is not yet a partner.

   D. Celizza, a human resources consultant for Mumbles who provided 5 hours of services to FTDI during the year under audit, and who is not yet a partner.

AICPA.101055AUD-SIM

36. Which of the following is an example of the type of threat to independence that the AICPA's conceptual framework anticipates in its rules?

   A. ABC Auditing prepared source documents for client XYZ Co. that were ultimately audited by ABC.
   B. ABC Auditing acted as a promoter of audit client XYZ Co.'s stock in an initial public offering.
   C. ABC Auditing's audit partner in charge of the XYZ Co. audit learned that her spouse had been promoted from a nonmanagerial role to CFO at XYZ.
   D. All three choices provided.

AICPA.101057AUD-SIM

37. The Melancon accounting firm audits XYZ Co. out of its Boston office. Who, among the following Melancon employees, is a "covered member" regarding XYZ?

   A. Sim, the receptionist who handles many administrative tasks for the XYZ audit team.
   B. Tim, the records guy who lugs around many, many boxes of records that the audit team must review.
   C. Bit, the new college accounting graduate, who was added to the XYZ audit team on his first day at Melancon.
   D. None of the three choices provided.

Network Firms and Affiliates

aq.network.firms.001_17

38. The Bilbao accounting firm audited Logan Co. and acquired the Seedman accounting firm, which provided internal audit services to Logan Co. Which of the following steps need **not** be taken to avoid impairing Bilbao's independence relative to Logan Co.?

   A. Seedman must stop providing internal audit services to Logan Co. before the acquisition is closed.
   B. Seedman employees who provided the internal audit services must not serve on the new firm's audit team for Logan.
   C. A threats and safeguards evaluation must be conducted to determine whether threats to independence have been reduced to an acceptable level.
   D. Any employees providing internal audit services to Logan must be fired.

AICPA.141027AUD-SIM

39. Which of the following is (are) true?

    A. If Firm A and Firm B are in the same network, A must be independent of B's attest clients if use of the audit or review reports is unrestricted.

    B. If Firm A and Firm B are in the same network, A must be independent of B's attest clients if use of the audit or review reports is restricted.

    C. Firms may never use partners or professional employees of other firms on their audit teams.

    D. All three answer choices provided are true.

AICPA.141028AUD-SIM

40. Which of the following are "affiliates" of clients so that a member in public practice might have to worry about its relationships with the entity in order to preserve independence?

    A. The Dawes accounting firm is auditing ABC Co., which owns 61% of the stock of DEF Mfg. Co. (from which Dawes has borrowed quite a bit of money.

    B. The Dawes accounting firm is auditing DEF Co., which is owned substantially by ABC Mfg. Co. (from which Dawes has borrowed quite a bit of money).

    C. The Dawes accounting firm is auditing ABC Co. and has borrowed quite a bit of money from DEF Mfg. Co. while the Pensive Hedge Fund owns a majority control of both ABC and DEF.

    D. All three answer choices provided.

Reissues, Engagement Letters, ADR, and Unpaid Fees

aq.reissue.eng.001_17

41. Which of the following terms would be properly included in an engagement letter signed by audit firm MNO and its client, Magnifica Corporation?

    A. MNO promises to reimburse Magnifica for any losses sustained by the wrongdoing of its own employees that MNO did not detect.

    B. Magnifica promises to reimburse MNO for any damages it must pay to investors caused by MNO's careless acts in conducting the Magnifica audit.

    C. Magnifica promises to reimburse MNO for any damages MNO must pay to investors caused by its nonnegligent failure to detect fraud by Magnifica's management.

    D. Neither MNO nor Magnifica will be liable to investors for any losses caused by their mutual errors that lead to the filing of materially erroneous financial statements.

AICPA.141020AUD-SIM

42. The Cheng Accounting Firm is concerned with litigation costs, so it is inserting provisions in all its engagement letters that require arbitration rather than litigation of disputes between Cheng and its attest clients. Which of the following is true?

    I. Such a provision is simply not allowed by the code.

    II. Such a provision is allowed, but if it is invoked, Cheng should apply the Conceptual Framework to determine whether independence is impaired by the fact that it and its client have potentially been placed in positions of material adverse interests.

    A. I only.

    B. II only.

    C. Both I and II.

    D. Neither I nor II.

AICPA.141021AUD-SIM

43. The Espinoza Accounting Firm is set to certify the financial statements of client ABC Co. on May 15, 2020. However, ABC did not pay Espinoza's bill for doing the previous audit that was signed on May 15, 2019. Which of the following is true?

    A. Because ABC has not paid Espinoza in more than a year, Espinoza's independence would be impaired if it signed this new report in 2020.

    B. Espinoza can avoid any independence problems by simply not billing ABC, which cannot be behind on its bills if it has not received any bills.

    C. Espinoza's independence would not be impaired if ABC would issue to it a signed note, promising to pay within six months.

    D. ABC's independence considerations should prevent it from signing the May 15, 2020, report even if ABC is in bankruptcy.

Financial Interests

Overview and Unsolicited Financial Interests

aq.over.fin.interest.001_17

44. Lil is on her firm's audit team for MNO Corporation. She receives notice that her rich aunt Sephora has died and left her stock in MNO. The will is in probate and probably will be for a few months. Which of the following steps are **not** steps that Lil should take to preserve independence?

   A. Dispose of the shares within 30 days of gaining the right to do so.
   B. Not participate in the engagement after learning of the interest and before disposing of it.
   C. Not purchase more MNO shares.
   D. Resign immediately from her firm and hope to be rehired in the following year.

aq.partner.529s.001_17

45. Member Sam is an auditor, but he also has investments in several different businesses. In which of these is his interest in XYZ Co. **not** direct?

   A. Sam is a general partner in the ABC Construction Company which, in turn, has invested some of its extra cash in XYZ Co.
   B. Sam is a limited partner in the DEF Cleaning Company which, in turn, has invested some of its extra cash in XYZ Co. Sam is a member of DEF's investment committee.
   C. Sam is a member of the GHI LLC, a member-managed limited liability company that has invested some of its extra cash in XYZ Co.
   D. Sam is a member of the JKL LLC, an agent-managed limited liability company that has invested some of its extra cash in XYZ Co.

AICPA.111159AUD

46. A CPA purchased stock in a client corporation and placed it in a trust as an educational fund for the CPA's minor child. The trust securities are not material to the CPA's wealth but are material to the child's personal net worth. According to the AICPA Code of Professional Conduct, would this action impair the CPA's independence with the client?

   A. No, because the CPA would not have a direct financial interest in the client.
   B. Yes, because the stock would be a direct financial interest and materiality is a factor.
   C. Yes, because the stock would be an indirect financial interest and materiality is not a factor.
   D. Yes, because the stock would be a direct financial interest and materiality is not a factor.

Mutual Funds and Retirement Plans

AICPA.141029AUD-SIM

47. Jo is a member in public practice who is very wealthy and has no individual investments that are material to her. Which of the following investments would impair Jo's independence?

   A. Jo owns 3% of a diversified mutual fund and is on her firm's attest team for that fund.
   B. Jo owns 4% of a diversified mutual fund and is on her firm's attest team for ABC Co., whose shares are in the mutual fund's portfolio of stocks.
   C. Jo owns 2% of an undiversified mutual fund that has ABC Co. stock in its portfolio (and Jo is on her firm's attest team for ABC).
   D. All three of the choices provided.

AICPA.141031AUD-SIM

48. Which of the following creates an independence problem?

   I. Sally participates in her firm's retirement plan, which allows her to select which companies' stocks go into her portfolio. Sally selects a small amount of ABC Co. stock, even though she is on her firm's audit team for ABC.
   II. Although Sally has not selected ABC Co. stock for her retirement plan's portfolio, her spouse, Joe, has done so.

   A. I only.
   B. II only.
   C. Both I and II.
   D. Neither I nor II.

Partnerships, 529s, Trust and Estates, Employee Benefit Plans

AICPA.141022AUD-SIM

49. Art is on his firm's audit team for client ABC Co. Which of the following is an indirect financial interest?

   A. Art is a general partner in a partnership that owns stock in ABC.
   B. Art is a limited partner in a partnership that owns stock in ABC and is on the partnership's investments committee.
   C. Art is a member in a member-managed limited liability corporation that owns stock in ABC.
   D. Art is a member in an agent-managed limited liability corporation that owns stock in ABC.

AICPA.141023AUD-SIM

50. The Lox Accounting Firm audits ABC Co. Pim is a Lox tax partner in the office that runs the ABC audit. Pim has been asked to be a trustee of an estate that has ABC stock in its portfolio. In which of the following situations would there be an independence problem for Lox?

   A. Pim has authority to make investment decisions for the estate.
   B. The estate owns more than 10% of ABC stock.
   C. More than 10% of the estate's assets are invested in ABC stock.
   D. All three choices provided.

Depository Accounts, Brokerage Accounts, and Insurance Policies

aq.depos.accts.001_17

51. Member Spencer maintains a brokerage account at TYD Brokers. Spencer was just named to his firm's audit team to the TYD account. Spencer is therefore deeply concerned about his independence. Which of the following is **true**?

   A. To be independent, Spencer must close his account at TYD and move to another broker.
   B. To be independent, Spencer need ensure only that TYD renders services to him on the same terms and conditions as to other customers.
   C. To be independent, Spencer need ensure only that any assets he has in the account that are subject to risk of loss are immaterial to his net worth.
   D. To be independent, Spencer must ensure **both** that TYD renders services to him on the same terms and conditions as to other customers **and** that any assets he has in the account that are subject to risk of loss are immaterial to his net worth.

AICPA.141035AUD-SIM

52. The Patton Accounting Firm and one of its partners, Tilly, have depository accounts at the ABC Bank. ABC has just approached Patton about becoming the bank's auditor. In which of the following situations would there be an independence problem if Patton became ABC's auditor?

   A. ABC is in robust financial health.
   B. Tilly's account is fully insured.
   C. Tilly's account is not fully insured, but the uninsured amount is not material to her financial situation.
   D. None of the three choices provided.

AICPA.141037AUD-SIM

53. Which of the following situations creates an independence problem for Kim?

   I. Kim owns an insurance policy that does not contain an investment option and was issued under normal terms, procedures, and requirements.
   II. Kim owns an insurance policy with an investment option, and she invested a small amount in the ABC Mutual Fund, even though Kim is a covered member for purposes of ABC, which is an audit client of her firm.

   A. I only.
   B. II only.
   C. Both I and II.
   D. Neither I nor II.

Loans, Leases, and Business Relationships

aq.loans.leases.001_17

54. Morgun is an audit partner at Ernst & Deloitte (E&D). One of Morgun's audit clients is Beezle Corporation, which is 100% owned by Dilbily. Morgun must, of course, be concerned about independence. Which of the following situations would **not** create an independence problem for Morgun?

   A. Morgun and Dilbily both own shares of Google.
   B. Morgun and Beezle both own 40% of a small manufacturing company in town.
   C. Morgun and Dilbily both love to ski and co-own a ski chalet near Aspen.
   D. Morgun and Dilbily both hate to ski but co-own a ski chalet near Aspen as an investment.

aq.loans.leases.002_17

55. Lynn is on the attest engagement team for Whillikers Manufacturing Corporation (WMC). Which of the following financial arrangements would **not** create an independence problem for Lynn?

   A. Lynn borrows $1,000 from Sam, an officer of WMC.
   B. Lynn loans $2,000 to Gonzo, an investor who owns 22% of WMC's outstanding shares.
   C. Lynn borrows $5,000 from WMC.
   D. Lynn considers asking WMC's CEO for a loan, but decides not to.

AICPA.080967REG-1B

56. Tondry is a CPA working for a Big Four firm as an auditor. Tondry has purchased a small minority interest in XYZ Co., which provides technical computer support and other nonaudit services for businesses. At least one of the businesses that receives technical support from XYZ (and purchases software on XYZ's recommendation for which XYZ received a commission), is an audit client for which Tondry is on the audit engagement team. Given these facts, which of the following is true?

   I. Tondry's actions have created an independence problem.
   II. The employees and agents of XYZ must follow independence rules just as Tondry must.

   A. I only.
   B. II only.
   C. I and II.
   D. Neither I nor II.

AICPA.141033AUD-SIM

57. The Bilton Accounting Firm needs office space, and ABC Co. has office space to lease out. ABC is an attest client of Bilton. Which of the following would **not** create an independence problem?

   A. ABC signs a capital lease agreement with Bilton on terms and conditions that are comparable with other leases in the area.
   B. ABC signs an operating lease with Bilton on terms and conditions that are comparable with other leases in the area, and Bilton is always on time with its payments.
   C. ABC signs an operating lease with Bilton that gives it a 10% discount from what ABC charges its other tenants.
   D. All three of the choices provided.

AICPA.141034AUD-SIM

58. Which of the following situations does not create an independence problem for the Brixton Accounting Firm relative to its attest client ABC Co.

   A. Both Brixton and ABC Co. own Microsoft stock.
   B. Both Brixton and ABC Co. purchase major stakes in a local technology start-up company.
   C. One of Brixton's covered members is friends with ABC's chief executive officer, and they pursue their passion for skiing by jointly purchasing a ski chalet in Vail.
   D. None of the above create an independence problem.

Family Relationships

aq.fam.relations.001_17

59. Wiley works for the Imlauf Accounting Firm. He is a tax partner in the Peoria office. The Bradley Manufacturing Co. (BMC) is an audit client of the Peoria office of Imlauf. Wiley provides more than 10 hours of tax advisory services to BMC each year. Wiley's spouse, Karen, works for Spiggot Corporation and participates in its employee benefit plan which holds a lot of BMC shares. Regarding Wiley's independence and the BMC audit, which of the following is **not** true?

   A. This arrangement is okay as long as Karen did not have any other benefit plan opportunities with Spiggot.
   B. This arrangement is okay as long as Karen divests herself of any interest in BMC should that opportunity arise under Spiggot's plan.
   C. This arrangement is okay, but if Wiley took up auditing and joined the audit team for BMC, problems would arise.
   D. Someone in Karen's shoes may never hold a material, indirect interest in a firm that her IFM is a covered member for.

AICPA.080925REG-1B

60. Anchorage Alltime Dairy (AAD) is an audit client of Thorn Granton's Juneau office. Al is on the audit team. Betsy evaluates Al's work and determines his pay. Carol is a tax professional in the Juneau office, who provided 20 hours of tax advice to AAD during the last audit cycle. Dave is a tax partner in the Juneau office, who has never provided any services to AAD. Which of the following situations would create an independence problem under the new AICPA rules?

   A. Al's brother Sam is in charge of manure disposal for AAD.
   B. Betsy's live-in lover owns enough AAD stock that it is material to him, but it does not allow him to exert significant influence over AAD.
   C. Carol's mother is a receptionist for AAD and, via its pension plan, indirectly owns a small amount of AAD stock.
   D. None of the choices provided.

AICPA.141006AUD-SIM

61. Which of the following is *not* an immediate family member?

   A. A covered member's spouse.
   B. A covered member's spousal equivalent.
   C. A covered member's nondependent child.
   D. A covered member's dependent stepson.

AICPA.141007AUD-SIM

62. Which of the following is *not* a close relative?

    A. A parent.
    B. A spousal equivalent.
    C. A sister.
    D. A nondependent child.

Employment Relationships

Current Employment

AICPA.060648REG

63. Under the ethical standards of the profession, which of the following business relationships would generally **not** impair an auditor's independence?

    A. Promoter of a client's securities.
    B. Member of a client's board of directors.
    C. Client's general counsel.
    D. Advisor to a client's board of trustees.

Subsequent Employment

AICPA.111157AUD

64. An issuer may hire an employee of a registered public accounting firm who served on the audit engagement team within the previous year for which of the following positions?

    A. Controller.
    B. CFO.
    C. CEO.
    D. Staff accountant.

AICPA.120604AUD

65. A cooling-off period of how many years is required before a member of an issuer's audit engagement team may begin working for the registrant in a key position?

    A. One year.
    B. Two years.
    C. Three years.
    D. Four years.

Other Associations and Relationships

aq.other.relations.001_17

66. Solly is a tax partner for the Duval Accounting Firm. She does not live in a convent. She interacts with the world. Which of the following is **not** true?

    A. Solly may join the Pleasant View Country Club, which is an audit client of Duval. So long as she joins primarily to play golf, independence is not impaired.
    B. Solly may buy a unit in the Last Days Condominium complex, even if Duval audits the condo association for the complex. Independence would not be impaired so long as several safeguards are met, such as Solly's annual assessment is not material to either her or the association, and sale of the association's common assets would not result in a distribution to Solly.
    C. Solly may join the Naval Credit Union in her community, even if the credit union is a Duval audit client. Independence would not be impaired if Solly qualified to join the credit union because her father had a 30-year career in the Navy.
    D. Solly may not accept a $100 ceramic frog from the Local Food Pantry, an audit client of Duval. Independence would be impaired by this gift even if Solly was a long-time volunteer at this food kitchen for the homeless that wished to honor Solly for 10 years of volunteering and knew that she collected frogs of various types.

AICPA.141039AUD-SIM

67. Which of the following safeguards must be met for Sam, who is a member of his condominium association, to be able to serve as a covered member of his firm, which audits the condominium association, without impairing independence?

    A. Sam's annual assessment must not be material to him or to the association.
    B. If the condominium association were liquidated, Sam would not receive a distribution.
    C. The condominium association's creditors would not be able to successfully sue Sam to recover his personal assets if the association became insolvent.
    D. All of the three choices provided.

AICPA.141040AUD-SIM

68. Which categories of covered members must be concerned with independence problems that might arise from gifts they receive from attest clients?

   I. Team members.
   II. Other partners in the office.

   A. I only.
   B. II only.
   C. Both I and II.
   D. Neither I nor II.

Nonaudit Services

Code Provisions

aq.code.prov.002_17

69. Sipta knows that her audit firm should not perform management responsibilities for audit clients. Which of the following is an example of a permitted activity?

   A. Setting strategic direction for the client.
   B. Preparing source documents that evidence occurrence of a transaction.
   C. Recommending a job description for a position that the client needs to fill.
   D. Taking custody of client assets.

aq.code.prov.003_17

70. The Pilden accounting firm wishes to sell some NAS to privately-held audit client Dimsdale Corporation. Which of the following is **not** true regarding independence rules for provision of NAS?

   A. Pilden should require that Dimsdale's management agrees to assume all management responsibilities, to oversee the service, to evaluate the adequacy and results of the services Pilden performs, and to accept responsibility for the results of the NAS.
   B. Pilden must not only avoid assuming management responsibilities itself, it also must assure itself that Dimsdale's managers are able to assume management responsibilities and oversee the services, make an informed judgment on the results of the NAS, and accept responsibility for making the judgments and decisions that are the proper responsibility of management.
   C. Pilden must establish and document in writing its understanding with Dimsdale regarding the objectives of

the engagement, the services to be performed, the Dimsdale's acceptance of responsibilities, Pilden's responsibilities, and any limitations on the engagement.
   D. Pilden should never attend a Dimsdale board meeting, even as just nonvoting advisor.

AICPA.141001AUD-SIM

71. Which of the following would be deemed by the code "management responsibilities" that would likely impair independence if a covered member performed them for an attest client?

   A. Setting policy or strategic direction for the attest client.
   B. Taking custody of client assets.
   C. Preparing source documents that evidence the occurrence of a transaction.
   D. All of the choices provided.

AICPA.141002AUD-SIM

72. Which of the following are considered by the code to be nonaudit services that could impair independence if performed by a covered member for an attest client?

   A. Discussing with the client selection and application of accounting standards or policies.
   B. Discussing with the client the appropriateness of the client's methods used to determine accounting and financial reporting.
   C. Discussing with the client the form or content of the financial statements.
   D. None of the choices provided.

AICPA.141004AUD-SIM

73. The Flakel Accounting Firm audits ABC Co., a public company. ABC would like to fire its current tax consultant and replace it with Flakel. Which of the following is true?

   I. This action would necessarily violate the Code.
   II. This action would violate Sarbanes-Oxley rules, unless ABC's audit committee preapproved the hiring.
   III. This action would violate Sarbanes-Oxley rules even if ABC's audit committee preapproved the hiring.

   A. I only.
   B. II only.
   C. III only.
   D. I and II.

Specific Services

aq.spec.serv.0001_0318

74. The Harvey CPA Firm prepared all tax returns for its attest client, Cary Corporation. Which of the following activities by Harvey would impair independence?

   A. At Cary's request, Harvey delivers copies of Cary's tax returns to ABC Co., which is considering investing in Cary.
   B. Harvey keeps copies of Cary's expense records that it used to prepare Cary's tax return.
   C. Harvey retains for its own records a copy of Cary's final tax return that Harvey prepared.
   D. Because Harvey has been Cary's tax accountant for years and expects to be so into the future, it retains many of the original underlying financial, business, and legal documents on Cary's behalf.

AICPA.141049AUD-SIM

75. Which of the following benefit plan administration services may not be provided by an auditor to a private company attest client?

   A. Communicate summary plan data to plan trustee.
   B. Advice client management regarding impact of plan provisions.
   C. Prepare account valuations.
   D. Make disbursements on plan's behalf.

AICPA.141051AUD-SIM

76. Which of the following internal audit functions may be performed by an auditor for a private company attest client?

   A. Reporting to the board on behalf of management regarding internal audit affairs.
   B. Identifying opportunities for improvement.
   C. Determining which, if any, recommendations for improving internal control systems should be implemented.
   D. Performing ongoing monitoring activities that affect execution of transactions.

Members in Business

aq.memb.bus.001_17

77. Which of the following actions by a MIBB would **not** threaten integrity or objectivity standards, or both?

   A. Jessie was an internal auditor for the privately-held Jonass Co. and on her birthday she accepted a gift from her company's external auditor in the form of a coffee mug emblazoned with the PriceToucheHouse logo.
   B. Surabi allowed her supervisor to pressure her into characterizing the tax implications of a transaction their company consummated in a manner that is completely erroneous in her view.
   C. Rachel, who works in internal audit, hid some unflattering financial details from her employer's external auditor.
   D. Nicole, a staff accountant at Nickleby Corporation, ordered a subordinate to back-date an IRS document.

AICPA.141044AUD-SIM

78. Which of the following is **not** true regarding application of the Conceptual Framework for members in business?

   A. An adverse interest threat arises when a member in business sues her employer.
   B. A familiarity threat arises when a member in business hires a relative to work for his employer.
   C. A self-review threat arises when a member in business reviews some internal audit work that she herself performed before she was promoted to her current position.
   D. A familiarity threat arises when a member in business has a long association with an employer.

Other Members

AICPA.141046AUD-SIM

79. Who of the following is an "other member" for code purposes?

   A. Tim, who is a retired CPA.
   B. Tom, who is an unemployed CPA.
   C. Bill, who is a CPA currently working as a rodeo clown.
   D. All of the choices provided.

AICPA.141047AUD-SIM

80. Which of the following are discreditable acts that should not be performed by other members?

   A. Sexual harassment in employment.
   B. Soliciting disclosure of CPA exam questions.
   C. Failure to file a tax return.
   D. All of the listed answer choices.

AICPA.141048AUD-SIM

81. Which of the following is a duty owed by an "other member"?

    I. Duty to be independent in fact and appearance.
    II. Duty to avoid committing discreditable acts.

    A. I only.
    B. II only.
    C. I and II.
    D. Neither I nor II.

Requirements of SEC and PCAOB

Securities and Exchange Commission (SEC)

aq.aud.sec.005_2017

82. Which of the following employment relationships does **not** impair independence under SEC rules?

    A. The Badger audit firm audits ABC Co., a publicly traded company. Tam is on Badger's audit team for the audit. His sister is a direct report of the CFO of ABC.
    B. The Otter audit firm audits XYZ Co., a publicly traded company. Tim was on Otter's audit team for the audit last year, but just a few days after last year's audit was completed, Tim severed all ties with Otter and went to work as the controller at XYZ.
    C. The Weasel audit firm audits LMN Co., a publicly traded company. LMN's audit cycle runs from January 1 to December 31. Tom was on Weasel's audit team for the 2016 audit. He severed all ties with Weasel on March 1, 2017. Tom went to work in a significant accounting position at LMN on January 2, 2019.
    D. The Possum audit firm audits PQR Co., a publicly traded company. Max is lead partner on the PQR audit team. Max's sister Estrella is CFO of PQR. Max and his sister are estranged.

aq.sec.exch.com.002_2017

83. Which of the following persons are "close family members" for purposes of SEC independence rules?

    A. Tina, a 14-year-old whose mother is on her firm's audit engagement team for the ABC Co. audit.
    B. Tip, whose cousin Fred is the lead partner on the ABC Co. audit.
    C. Merlin, whose granddaughter just joined an accounting firm and is providing technical advice to the audit team doing the ABC Co. audit.

    D. Sam, whose best friend since childhood is Muhammad, who is on the audit team for the ABC Co. audit.

aq.sec.exch.com.003_2017

84. Which of the following financial investments is **not** likely to create an independence problem for Kim, who is a "covered person" at her accounting firm for purposes of the audit of ABC Co.?

    A. Kim owns 0.1% of ABC's outstanding shares.
    B. Kim owns 1% of XYZ Co., which in turn owns 40% of ABC's shares.
    C. Kim owns 5% of an undiversified mutual fund that has a significant investment in ABC.
    D. Kim is a trustee of the Melon Trust. The trust owns a few shares of ABC, but Kim had nothing to do with that acquisition and, indeed, has no authority to make investment decisions for the trust.

aq.sec.exch.com.004_2017

85. Which of the following transactions impairs independence under the SEC rules?

    A. The Lark audit firm audits ABC Co., a Fortune 100 company that manufactures widgets. Pam, who is on Lark's audit team, borrows money from ABC to buy a car. The loan is collateralized by the automobile.
    B. The Wren audit firm audits XYZ Co., a publicly traded financial institution. Pim, who is on Wren's audit team, has a credit card issued by XYZ and currently owes $20,000 on the card.
    C. The Meadowlark audit firm audits LMN Co., a publicly traded insurance company, which is teetering on the brink of bankruptcy. Pom is on Meadowlark's audit team for the LMN audit and owns a life insurance policy issued by Pom that she bought before she became a covered person.
    D. All of the options.

aq.sec.exch.com.006_17

86. Which of the following relationships is permitted under SEC independence rules?

    A. ABC Accounting Firm audits DEF Co., a large public company. Before DEF became an audit client, several ABC partners bought small amounts of DEF stock. Cumulatively, they own 6.3% of DEF stock and have not sold it.
    B. Susie is on GHI Accounting Firm's audit engagement team for client JKL Co., a large public corporation. Susie's spouse is on JKL's board of directors.

C. Timmy is a tax partner in,the Akron office of the MNO Accounting Firm, which has as an audit client PQR Co., a large public corporation. Timmy does 15 hours of tax work for PQR every year and owns some shares of PQR stock.

D. Mary is an auditor at the STU Accounting Firm which has as an audit client VWX Corp., a large public banking company. Mary is not on the audit team for VWX, but before she ever went to work for STU, she borrowed money from VWX for buy her car. The loan is still outstanding, but it is collateralized by the car and Mary's payments are up-to-date.

Public Company Accounting Oversight Board (PCAOB)

aq.aud.pcaob.001_2017

87. The Niblock accounting firm audited JFK, Inc., a public company. Niblock also provided tax services to JFK, receiving as its fee 20% of any tax savings JFK enjoyed because of Niblock's advice. Which of the following is true?

A. Tax advice to a public company audit client is automatically forbidden and impairs independence.

B. This tax advice impairs independence because of the nature of the tax advice given.

C. This tax advice impairs independence because it was provided on a contingent fee basis.

D. If the contingent fee had been only 10%, it would have been fine.

aq.aud.pcaob.002_2017

88. Whether seeking an audit committee's permission to provide permissible tax services or other non-audit services to a public company audit client or when preparing to take a public company on as a new audit client, three important steps are:

A. Describe, discuss, and document.

B. Request, explain, and record.

C. Seek, document, and reconsider.

D. Describe, examine, and reexamine.

aq.aud.pcaob.003_2017

89. The Single accounting firm audits Double, Inc., a public company. Which of the following people may **not** receive any tax service consulting from Single?

A. Bill, who is an outside director on Double's board.

B. Omar, Double's head of internal audit.

C. Kelly, Double's controller, who was hired away from a competitor in the middle of an audit cycle when the former controller died suddenly and the contract to provide the tax advice was assigned before Kelly joined Double and the services were terminated 39 days after Kelly began work.

D. Sally, assistant CFO of a Double subsidiary that is audited by Triple accounting firm.

Requirements of GAO and DOL

Government Accounting Office (GAO)

aq.gao.001

90. A government internal audit function is presumed to be free from organizational independence impairments for reporting internally when the head of the organization:

A. Is not accountable to those charged with governance.

B. Performs auditing procedures that are consistent with generally accepted accounting principles.

C. Is a line-manager of the unit under audit.

D. Is removed from political pressures to conduct audits objectively, without fear of political reprisal.

aq.gao.002

91. Which of the following services would constitute a management function under Government Auditing Standards, and result in the impairment of a CPA's independence if performed by the CPA?

A. Developing entity program policies.

B. Providing methodologies, such as practice guides.

C. Providing accounting opinions to a legislative body.

D. Recommending internal control procedures.

AICPA.101018AUD-SIM

92. Sue's firm was hired to audit a Reno County project that used federal grant money to attempt to create jobs for people on welfare. Sue was in charge of the audit, and her team found many questionable practices. When the chief administrator of Reno County's government heard about Sue's preliminary findings, he called her into his office and told her that her firm would lose every single audit contract it had with every single unit of Reno County government if he was not pleased with Sue's audit report. This is an example of:

   A. A potential personal impairment of independence.

   B. A potential external impairment of independence.

   C. A potential organizational impairment of independence.

   D. None of the above.

AICPA.101019AUD-SIM

93. The City of Fairluth's internal auditor became ill, which created some difficult situations. Chiang typically audited Fairluth on behalf of his accounting firm. When the mayor prevailed upon Chiang to temporarily help prepare the city's basic financial records, he did so. Later, he and his team audited those records and pronounced them fair and accurate. And they probably were. Nonetheless, is it possible that we have an independence problem here under GAO guidelines regarding nonaudit services?

   A. No, this was an emergency situation and Chiang acted sensibly in a manner that does not implicate independence rules so that supplemental safeguards need even be considered.

   B. No, this activity did raise independence issues, but they are easily remedied by resort to supplemental safeguards such as ensuring that extent of the audit work was not reduced below that which is normal.

   C. Yes, this activity raises independence problems that are so severe that they cannot be remedied by application of supplemental safeguards.

   D. None of the above.

AICPA.101136AUD-SIM

94. The GAO's independence rules for auditing apply when Sam audits which of the following:

   A. IBM.

   B. The Corner Store, a small business opened by two recent immigrants.

   C. Maricopa County, Arizona.

   D. All of the above.

Department of Labor (DOL)

AICPA.101014AUD-SIM

95. The ABC Accounting firm is auditing an employee benefit plan. Which of the following parties cannot have any direct or material indirect financial interest in the plan to prevent an independence violation?

   A. A member of the engagement team.

   B. A partner in an office in another city.

   C. ABC itself.

   D. A, B, and C.

AICPA.101015AUD-SIM

96. Tim is an auditor helping to audit an employee benefit plan. Which of the following roles connected to the plan would create independence problems for Tim if performed by a partner in his office?

   A. Promoter.

   B. Underwriter.

   C. Voting Trustee.

   D. All of the above.

AICPA.101016AUD-SIM

97. Wang is an auditor helping to audit an employee benefit plan. Which of the following services would create independence problems for Wang if performed by members of his office for the plan?

   A. Maintaining financial records.

   B. Performing actuarial services.

   C. Advising on tax issues.

   D. All of the above.

assess.AICPA.AUD.dol-0023

98. According to the U.S. Department of Labor, an auditor of an employee benefit plan would be considered independent if

   A. The auditor is committed to acquire a material indirect financial interest in the plan sponsor.

   B. An actuary associated with the auditor's firm renders services to the plan.

   C. A member of the auditor's firm is an investment advisor to the plan.

   D. The auditor's firm maintains financial records for the plan.

Assessing Risk and Developing a Planned Response

Financial Statement Audits

Accounting vs. Auditing

aq.acct.aud.001_2017

99. Which of the following is not a primary responsibility of an auditor:

   A. Provide regulators with an opinion on whether the financial statements are presented fairly, in all material respects, in accordance with the applicable financial reporting framework.
   B. Provide creditors with an opinion on whether the financial statements are presented fairly, in all material respects, in accordance with the applicable financial reporting framework.
   C. Provide management with an opinion on whether the financial statements are presented fairly, in all material respects, in accordance with the applicable financial reporting framework.
   D. Provide investors with an opinion by the auditor on whether the financial statements are presented fairly, in all material respects, in accordance with the applicable financial reporting framework.

GAAS and Principles

AICPA.090780.AUD-AU

100. According to GAAS, which of the following terms identifies a requirement for audit evidence?

   A. Appropriate.
   B. Adequate.
   C. Reasonable.
   D. Disconfirming.

AICPA.101119AUD

101. An independent auditor must have which of the following?

   A. A pre-existing and well-informed point of view with respect to the audit.
   B. Technical training that is adequate to meet the requirements of a professional.
   C. A background in many different disciplines.
   D. Experience in taxation that is sufficient to comply with generally accepted auditing standards.

AICPA.900547AUD-AU

102. The exercise of due professional care requires that an auditor

   A. Examine all available corroborating evidence.
   B. Critically review the judgment exercised at every level of supervision.
   C. Reduce control risk below the maximum.
   D. Attain the proper balance of professional experience and formal education.

Professional Standards

AICPA.130506AUD-SIM

103. Interpretive publications include all of the following, except for

   A. Appendices to Statements on Auditing Standards.
   B. Articles in the AICPA's *Journal of Accountancy*.
   C. Auditing guidance included in AICPA Audit and Accounting Guides.
   D. Auditing interpretations of the Statements on Auditing Standards.

AICPA.130507AUD-SIM

104. In AICPA professional standards, the word *should* indicates an (a)

   A. Interpretive suggestion that does not constitute a professional requirement.
   B. Unconditional requirement with which the auditor is obligated to comply.
   C. Presumptively mandatory requirement from which the CPA may depart in rare circumstances.
   D. Recommendation that has no authoritative status.

Quality Control Standards (SQCS)

AICPA.111173AUD

105. Which of the following actions should a CPA firm take to comply with the AICPA's quality control standards?

   A. Establish procedures that comply with the standards of the Sarbanes-Oxley Act.
   B. Use attributes sampling techniques in testing internal controls.
   C. Consider inherent risk and control risk before determining detection risk.
   D. Establish policies to ensure that the audit work meets applicable professional standards.

AICPA.911101AUD-AU

106. A CPA firm would be reasonably assured of meeting its responsibility to provide services that conform with professional standards by

   A. Adhering to generally accepted auditing standards.
   B. Having an appropriate system of quality control.
   C. Joining professional societies that enforce ethical conduct.
   D. Maintaining an attitude of independence in its engagements.

AICPA.921103AUD-AU

107. One of a CPA's firm's basic objectives is to provide professional services that conform with professional standards.

   Reasonable assurance of achieving this basic objective is provided through

   A. A system of quality control.
   B. A system of peer review.
   C. Continuing professional education.
   D. Compliance with generally accepted reporting standards.

assess.AICPA.AUD.sqcs-0010

108. How should differences of opinion between the engagement partner and the quality control reviewer be resolved?

   A. By adhering to industry best practices.
   B. By following the firm's policies and procedures.
   C. By accepting the recommendations of the client's audit committee.
   D. By issuing a disclaimer of opinion and reporting the issue to those charged with the entity's governance.

Overview of Audit Process

AICPA.901116AUD-AU-SIM

109. Principles Underlying an Audit Conducted in Accordance with GAAS state that sufficient appropriate audit evidence is to be obtained through designing and implementing appropriate responses, i.e., by performing audit procedures, to afford a reasonable basis for an opinion regarding the financial statements under audit. The substantive evidential matter required by this standard may be obtained, in part, through

   A. Flowcharting the internal control structure.
   B. Proper planning of the audit engagement.
   C. Analytical procedures.
   D. Audit documentation.

AICPA.940503AUD-AU

110. The audit work performed by each assistant should be reviewed to determine whether it was adequately performed and to evaluate whether the

   A. Auditor's system of quality control has been maintained at a high level.
   B. Results are consistent with the conclusions to be presented in the auditor's report.
   C. Audit procedures performed are approved in the professional standards.
   D. Audit has been performed by persons having adequate technical training and proficiency as auditors.

Overview of Auditor's Report

AICPA.100984AUD-AU-SIM

111. The auditor makes explicit reference to "auditing standards generally accepted in the United States of America" in which paragraph of the standard unmodified audit report?

   A. Opening.
   B. Auditor's Responsibility.
   C. Opinion.
   D. Both B and C.

AICPA.901107AUD-AU-SIM

112. GAAS require the auditor's report to contain either an expression of opinion regarding the financial statements or an assertion to the effect that an opinion cannot be expressed. The objective of this requirement is to prevent

   A. Misinterpretations regarding the degree of responsibility the auditor is assuming.
   B. An auditor from reporting on one basic financial statement and not the others.

C. An auditor from expressing different opinions on each of the basic financial statements.

D. Restrictions on the scope of the examination, whether imposed by the client, or by the inability to obtain evidence.

AICPA.911121AUD-AU

113. How does an auditor make the following representations when issuing the standard auditor's report on comparative financial statements?

	Examination of Evidence	Consistent Application of Accounting Principles
A.	Explicitly	Explicitly
B.	Implicitly	Implicitly
C.	Implicitly	Explicitly
D.	Explicitly	Implicitly

AICPA.920511AUD-AU-SIM

114. An auditor's responsibility to express an opinion on the financial statements is

A. Implicitly represented in the auditor's unmodified report.

B. Explicitly represented in the responsibility paragraphs of the auditor's unmodified report.

C. Explicitly represented in the opening paragraph of the auditor's unmodified report.

D. Explicitly represented in the opinion paragraph of the auditor's unmodified report.

Different Types of Engagements

AICPA.920560AUD-AU

115. An attestation engagement is one in which a CPA is engaged to

A. Issue a written communication expressing a conclusion about the reliability of a written assertion that is the responsibility of another party.

B. Provide tax advice or prepare a tax return based on financial information the CPA has not audited or reviewed.

C. Testify as an expert witness in accounting, auditing, or tax matters, given certain stipulated facts.

D. Assemble pro forma financial statements based on the representations of the entity's management without expressing any assurance.

AICPA.990403AUD-AU

116. An entity engaged a CPA to determine whether the client's web sites meet defined criteria for standard business practices and controls over transaction integrity and information protection.

In performing this engagement, the CPA should comply with the provisions of

A. Statements on Assurance Standards.

B. Statements on Standards for Attestation Engagements.

C. Statements on Standards for Management Consulting Services.

D. Statements on Auditing Standards.

PCAOB Responsibilities

AICPA.040214FAR-SIM

117. The Public Company Accounting Oversight Board (PCAOB) is charged with all of the following responsibilities except:

A. Establishing accounting standards for public companies.

B. Establishing auditing standards.

C. Registering accounting firms that will audit public companies.

D. Inspecting accounting firms that will audit public companies.

AICPA.101149AUD

118. Under the Sarbanes-Oxley Act of 2002, which of the following is **not** a stated responsibility of the Public Company Accounting Oversight Board?

A. Conducting inspections of registered public accounting firms.

B. Overseeing the registration of public accounting firms.

C. Issuing accounting standards that must be followed by issuers in financial reporting.

D. Issuing auditing standards that must be followed by registered public accounting firms in auditing the financial statements of issuers.

AICPA.101150AUD

119. The Sarbanes-Oxley Act of 2002 imposes a mandatory rotation applicable to both the audit engagement partner and the quality control (also called review) partner. How long in total is the partner allowed to serve as the engagement partner or review partner before someone else must serve in that capacity?

   A. 3 years.
   B. 5 years.
   C. 7 years.
   D. 10 years.

assess.AICPA.AUD.pcaob.resp-0043

120. At least how often should the PCAOB inspect a registered public accounting firm that regularly issues audit reports to 50 issuers?

   A. Annually.
   B. Every two years.
   C. Every three years.
   D. As requested by the firm.

PCAOB on Engagement Quality Review

AICPA.aq.pcaob.eng.qual.rev.001_18

121. According to PCAOB standards, each of the following items of information should be included in the documentation of an engagement quality review **except**

   A. Identification of the engagement quality reviewer and others who assisted the reviewer.
   B. Identification of the documents reviewed by the engagement quality reviewer and others who assisted the reviewer.
   C. The date on which the engagement quality reviewer provided concurring approval of issuance.
   D. An assessment by the engagement quality reviewer of the instances of fraud identified by the audit team.

AICPA.100979AUD-SIM

122. PCAOB standards applicable to an engagement quality review identify each of the following as examples of a "significant engagement deficiency," except for when

   A. The engagement team concluded that management's accounting estimates were unreasonable.
   B. The engagement team reached an inappropriate conclusion.
   C. The firm is not independent of its client.
   D. The engagement report is inappropriate.

AICPA.100980AUD-SIM

123. Which of the following is **not** a correct statement regarding differences between PCAOB auditing standards on engagement quality review and AICPA Statements on Quality Control Standards (SQCS)?

   A. PCAOB auditing standards require a concurring approval of issuance before the engagement report is released, whereas the SQCS have no such requirement.
   B. PCAOB auditing standards require a cooling-off period of at least two years before an engagement partner can serve as an engagement quality reviewer, whereas the SQCS have no such requirement.
   C. PCAOB auditing standards require engagement quality review documentation to be retained separately from the related engagement documentation for 10 years, whereas SQCS only require that the engagement quality review documentation be retained for 5 years with the other related engagement documentation.
   D. PCAOB auditing standards require an engagement quality review before an audit report is released, whereas SQCS do not require an engagement quality review.

AICPA.100981AUD-SIM

124. Which of the following statements is correct regarding characteristics required of an engagement quality reviewer under PCAOB auditing standards?

   A. Only a partner of the registered public accounting firm conducting the audit can serve as an engagement quality reviewer.
   B. An individual outside of the registered public accounting firm becomes an "associated person" of the registered public accounting firm when receiving compensation from the firm for performing the engagement quality review.
   C. There is no requirement that the engagement quality reviewer must be independent from the client involved, since the engagement quality reviewer cannot make engagement team decisions or otherwise assume any responsibilities of the engagement team.
   D. The engagement quality reviewer is required to be a partner in a public accounting firm, regardless of whether the reviewer is from within the firm or outside the firm responsible for the audit engagement subject to the engagement quality review.

AICPA.100982AUD-SIM

125. To evaluate the significant judgments and conclusions of the engagement team under PCAOB auditing standards, the engagement quality reviewer should

   A. Make inquiries of client personnel and perform analytical procedures.
   B. Perform tests of details and analytical procedures to corroborate client account balances.
   C. Make inquiries of client personnel and selected members of the engagement team.
   D. Discuss matters with members of the engagement team, including the engagement partner, and review engagement documentation.

Planning Activities

Pre-Engagement Planning Issues

AICPA.010502AUD-AU

126. Which of the following factors *most likely* would cause a CPA to not accept a new audit engagement?

   A. The prospective client has already completed its physical inventory count.
   B. The CPA lacks an understanding of the prospective client's operations and industry.
   C. The CPA is unable to review the predecessor auditor's documentation.
   D. The prospective client is unwilling to make all financial records available to the CPA.

AICPA.020403AUD-AU

127. An auditor's engagement letter *most likely* would include

   A. Management's acknowledgment of its responsibility for maintaining effective internal control.
   B. The auditor's preliminary assessment of the risk factors relating to misstatements arising from fraudulent financial reporting.
   C. A reminder that management is responsible for illegal acts committed by employees.
   D. A request for permission to contact the client's lawyer for assistance in identifying litigation, claims, and assessments.

AICPA.111170AUD

128. Before accepting an engagement to audit a new client, a CPA is required to obtain

   A. An assessment of fraud risk factors likely to cause material misstatements.
   B. An understanding of the prospective client's industry and business.
   C. The prospective client's signature to a written engagement letter.
   D. The prospective client's consent to make inquiries of the predecessor, if any.

AICPA.120716AUD

129. The understanding with the client regarding a financial statement audit generally includes which of the following matters?

   A. The audit plan identifying the nature, timing, and extent of planned audit procedures.
   B. The responsibilities of the auditor.
   C. The contingency fee structure.
   D. The preliminary judgment about materiality.

AICPA.130712AUD

130. Which of the following matters does an auditor usually include in the engagement letter?

   A. Arrangements regarding fees and billing.
   B. Analytical procedures that the auditor plans to perform.
   C. Indications of negative cash flows from operating activities.
   D. Identification of working capital deficiencies.

Planning and Supervision

AICPA.090753.AUD.AU

131. Which of the following could be difficult to determine because electronic evidence may not be retrievable after a specific period?

   A. The acceptance level of detection risk.
   B. The timing of control and substantive tests.
   C. Whether to adopt substantive or reliance test strategies.
   D. The assessed level of inherent risk.

AICPA.101116AUD

132. Which of the following conditions *most likely* would pose the greatest risk in accepting a new audit engagement?

   A. Staff will need to be rescheduled to cover this new client.
   B. There will be a client-imposed scope limitation.

C. The firm will have to hire a specialist in one audit area.

D. The client's financial reporting system has been in place for 10 years.

AICPA.101117AUD

133. Which of the following factors is *most likely* to affect the extent of the documentation of the auditor's understanding of a client's system of internal controls?

A. The industry and the business and regulatory environments in which the client operates.

B. The degree to which information technology is used in the accounting function.

C. The relationship between management, the board of directors, and external stakeholders.

D. The degree to which the auditor intends to use internal audit personnel to perform substantive tests.

AICPA.120712AUD

134. Which of the following procedures would an auditor *most likely* perform in the planning stage of an audit?

A. Make a preliminary judgment about materiality.

B. Confirm a sample of the entity's accounts payable with known creditors.

C. Obtain written representations from management that there are NO unrecorded transactions.

D. Communicate management's initial selection of accounting policies to the audit committee.

AICPA.980518AUD-AU

135. Which of the following procedures would an auditor *most likely* include in the planning phase of a financial statement audit?

A. Obtain an understanding of the entity's risk assessment process.

B. Identify specific internal control activities designed to prevent fraud.

C. Evaluate the reasonableness of the entity's accounting estimates.

D. Perform cutoff tests of the entity's sales and purchases.

Materiality

AICPA.101115AUD

136. An auditor finds several errors in the financial statements that the client prefers not to correct. The auditor determines that the errors are not material in the aggregate. Which of the following actions by the auditor is most appropriate?

A. Document the errors in the summary of uncorrected errors, and document the conclusion that the errors do **not** cause the financial statements to be misstated.

B. Document the conclusion that the errors do **not** cause the financial statements to be misstated, but do **not** summarize uncorrected errors in the audit documentation.

C. Summarize the uncorrected errors in the audit documentation, but do **not** document whether the errors cause the financial statements to be misstated.

D. Do **not** summarize the uncorrected errors in the audit documentation, and do **not** document a conclusion about whether the uncorrected errors cause the financial statements to be misstated.

AICPA.950511AUD-AU

137. Which of the following would an auditor *most likely* use in determining the auditor's preliminary judgment about materiality?

A. The anticipated sample size of the planned substantive tests.

B. The entity's annualized interim financial statements.

C. The results of the internal control questionnaire.

D. The contents of the management representation letter.

AICPA.970510AUD-AU

138. Which of the following would an auditor *most likely* use in determining the auditor's preliminary judgment about materiality?

A. The results of the initial assessment of control risk.

B. The anticipated sample size for planned substantive tests.

C. The entity's financial statements of the prior year.

D. The assertions that are embodied in the financial statements.

AICPA.980521AUD-AU

139. When issuing an unqualified opinion, the auditor who evaluates the audit findings should be satisfied that the

   A. Amount of known misstatement is documented in the management representation letter.
   B. Estimate of the total likely misstatement is less than a material amount.
   C. Amount of known misstatement is acknowledged and recorded by the client.
   D. Estimate of the total likely misstatement includes the adjusting entries already recorded by the client.

assess.AICPA.AUD.materiality-0011

140. Based on new information gained during an audit of a nonissuer, an auditor determines that it is necessary to modify materiality for the financial statements as a whole. In this circumstance, which of the following statements is accurate?

   A. The auditor is required to reperform audit procedures already completed on the audit using the revised materiality.
   B. The auditor should consider disclaiming an opinion due to a scope limitation.
   C. The revision of materiality at the financial statement levels will **not** affect the planned nature and timing of audit procedures, only the extent of those procedures.
   D. Materiality levels for particular classes of transactions, account balances, or disclosures might also need to be revised.

Audit Risk

AICPA.aq.aud.risk.001_17

141. As a result of control testing, a CPA has decided to reduce control risk. What is the impact on substantive testing sample size if all other factors remain constant?

   A. The sample size would be irrelevant.
   B. The sample size would be higher.
   C. The sample size would be lower.
   D. The sample size would be unaffected.

AICPA.130711AUD

142. Inherent risk and control risk differ from detection risk in which of the following ways?

   A. Inherent risk and control risk are calculated by the client.
   B. Inherent risk and control risk exist independently of the audit.

C. Inherent risk and control risk are controlled by the auditor.
D. Inherent risk and control risk exist as a result of the auditor's judgment about materiality.

AICPA.910526AUD-AU

143. The acceptable level of detection risk is inversely related to the

   A. Assurance provided by substantive tests.
   B. Risk of misapplying auditing procedures.
   C. Preliminary judgment about materiality levels.
   D. Risk of failing to discover material misstatements.

AICPA.911107AUD-AU

144. The risk that an auditor will conclude, based on substantive tests, that a material error does not exist in an account balance when, in fact, such error does exist is referred to as

   A. Sampling risk.
   B. Detection risk.
   C. Nonsampling risk.
   D. Inherent risk.

AICPA.920557AUD-AU

145. Inherent risk and control risk differ from detection risk in that inherent risk and control risk are

   A. Elements of audit risk while detection risk is not.
   B. Changed at the auditor's discretion while detection risk is not.
   C. Considered at the individual account-balance level while detection risk is not.
   D. Functions of the client and its environment while detection risk is not.

AICPA.921110AUD-AU

146. As the acceptable level of detection risk increases, an auditor may change the

   A. Assessed level of control risk from below the maximum to the maximum level.
   B. Assurance provided by tests of controls by using a larger sample size than planned.
   C. Timing of substantive tests from year end to an interim date.
   D. Nature of substantive tests from a less effective to a more effective procedure.

AICPA.940523AUD-AU

147. When an auditor increases the assessed level of control risk because certain control procedures were determined to be ineffective, the auditor would *most likely* increase the

   A. Extent of tests of controls.
   B. Level of detection risk.
   C. Extent of tests of details.
   D. Level of inherent risk.

AICPA.941108AUD-AU

148. Inherent risk and control risk differ from detection risk in that they

   A. Arise from the misapplication of auditing procedures.
   B. May be assessed in either quantitative or nonquantitative terms.
   C. Exist independently of the financial statement audit.
   D. Can be changed at the auditor's discretion.

AICPA.970511AUD-AU

149. Holding other planning considerations equal, a decrease in the number of misstatements in a class of transactions that an auditor could tolerate *most likely* would cause the auditor to

   A. Apply the planned substantive tests prior to the balance sheet date.
   B. Perform the planned auditing procedures closer to the balance sheet date.
   C. Increase the assessed level of control risk for relevant financial statement assertions.
   D. Decrease the extent of auditing procedures to be applied to the class of transactions.

Analytical Procedures

AICPA.aq.analytical.proc.001_17

150. An auditor who performed analytical procedures that compared current-year financial information to the comparable prior period noted a significant increase in net income. Given this result, which of the following expectations of recorded amounts would be unreasonable?

   A. A decrease in costs of goods sold as a percentage of sales.
   B. A decrease in accounts payable.
   C. A decrease in retained earnings.
   D. A decrease in notes payable.

AICPA.aq.analytical.proc.002_17

151. Which of the following results of analytical procedures would *most likely* indicate possible unrecorded liabilities?

   A. Current ratio of 2:1 as compared to 5:1 for the prior period.
   B. Ratio of accounts payable to total current liabilities of 4:1, compared to 6:1 for the prior period.
   C. Accounts payable turnover of 5, compared to 10 for the prior period.
   D. Accounts payable balance increase greater than 10% over the prior period.

AICPA.aq.analytical.proc.004_17

152. Which of the following procedures would an auditor *most likely* use to identify unusual year-end transactions?

   A. Obtaining a client representation letter.
   B. Obtaining a legal inquiry letter.
   C. Performing analytical procedures.
   D. Testing arithmetic accuracy of the accounting records.

AICPA.090746.AUD.AU

153. Which of the following *most likely* would cause an auditor to consider whether a client's financial statements contain material misstatements?

   A. Management did not disclose to the auditor that it consulted with other accountants about significant accounting matters.
   B. The chief financial officer will not sign the management representation letter until the last day of the auditor's fieldwork.
   C. Audit trails of computer-generated transactions exist only for a short time.
   D. The results of an analytical procedure disclose unexpected differences.

AICPA.090750.AUD.AU

154. Which of the following is an analytical procedure that an auditor *most likely* would perform when planning an audit?

   A. Confirming a sample of accounts payable.
   B. Scanning payroll files for terminated employees
   C. Comparing current-year balances to budgeted balances
   D. Recalculating interest expense based on notes payable balances

AICPA.111162AUD

155. A primary objective of analytical procedures used in the final review stage of an audit is to

A. Identify account balances that represent specific risks relevant to the audit.
B. Gather evidence from tests of details to corroborate financial statement assertions.
C. Detect fraud that may cause the financial statements to be misstated.
D. Assist the auditor in evaluating the overall financial statement presentation.

AICPA.111172AUD

156. Which of the following activities is an analytical procedure an auditor would perform in the final overall review stage of an audit to ensure that the financial statements are free from material misstatement?

A. Reading the minutes of the board of directors' meetings for the year under audit.
B. Obtaining a letter concerning potential liabilities from the client's attorney
C. Comparing the current year's financial statements with those of the prior year
D. Ensuring that a representation letter signed by management is in the file

AICPA.111185AUD

157. Which of the following statements is correct concerning analytical procedures used in planning an audit engagement?

A. They often replace the tests of controls that are performed to assess control risk.
B. They usually use financial and nonfinancial data aggregated at a high level.
C. They usually involve the comparison of assertions developed by management to ratios calculated by an auditor.
D. They are often used to develop an auditor's preliminary judgment about materiality.

AICPA.120703AUD

158. Which of the following would **not** be considered an analytical procedure?

A. Converting dollar amounts of income statement account balances to percentages of net sales for comparison with industry averages.
B. Developing the current year's expected net sales based on the sales trend of similar entities within the same industry
C. Projecting a deviation rate by comparing the results of a statistical sample with the actual population characteristics
D. Estimating the current year's expected expenses based on the prior year's expenses and the current year's budget

Detecting Fraud

AICPA.aq.det.fraud.001_17

159. What is the definition of fraud in an audit of financial statements?

A. An intentional act that results in a material misstatement in financial statements that are the subject of an audit.
B. The unintentional misapplication of accounting principles relating to amounts, classification, manner of presentation, or disclosure.
C. An intentional act that results in a material weakness in financial statements that are the subject of an audit.
D. Management's inability to design and implement programs and controls to prevent, deter, and detect material misstatements.

AICPA.010503AUD-AU

160. Which of the following factors would be *most likely* to heighten an auditor's concern about the risk of fraudulent financial reporting?

A. Large amounts of liquid assets that are easily convertible into cash.
B. Low growth and profitability as compared to other entities in the same industry.
C. Financial management's participation in the initial selection of accounting principles.
D. An overly complex organizational structure involving unusual lines of authority.

AICPA.020407AUD-AU

161. Which of the following circumstances *most likely* would cause an auditor to suspect that material misstatements exist in a client's financial statements?

A. The assumptions used in developing the prior year's accounting estimates have changed.
B. Differences between reconciliations of control accounts and subsidiary records are not investigated.
C. Negative confirmation requests yield fewer responses than in the prior year's audit.
D. Management consults with another CPA firm about complex accounting matters.

AICPA.111178AUD

162. Prior to, or in conjunction with, the information-gathering procedures for an audit, audit team members should discuss the potential for material misstatement due to fraud. Which of the following best characterizes the mindset that the audit team should maintain during this discussion?

   A. Presumptive.
   B. Judgmental.
   C. Criticizing
   D. Questioning.

AICPA.120711AUD

163. Which of the following situations *most likely* represents the highest risk of a misstatement arising from misappropriations of assets?

   A. A large number of bearer bonds on hand.
   B. A large number of inventory items with low sales prices.
   C. A large number of transactions processed in a short period of time.
   D. A large number of fixed assets with easily identifiable serial numbers.

AICPA.130717AUD

164. While performing an audit of the financial statements of a company for the year ended December 31, year 1, the auditor notes that the company's sales increased substantially in December, year 1, with a corresponding decrease in January, year 2. In assessing the risk of fraudulent financial reporting or misappropriation of assets, what should be the auditor's initial indication about the potential for fraud in sales revenue?

   A. There is a broad indication of misappropriation of assets.
   B. There is an indication of theft of the entity's assets.
   C. There is an indication of embezzling receipts.
   D. There is a broad indication of financial reporting fraud.

assess.AICPA.AUD.det.fraud-0036

165. An auditor of a nonissuer exercising professional skepticism with respect to the risks of material misstatement due to fraud will most appropriately

   A. Adopt an attitude of acceptance unless evidence indicates otherwise.
   B. Authenticate documents used as audit evidence.
   C. Consider the reliability of information to be used as audit evidence.
   D. Assess the entity's document-retention controls before using documents as audit evidence.

assess.AICPA.AUD.det.fraud-0039

166. Which of the following statements is correct with respect to fraud encountered during an audit engagement of a nonissuer?

   A. The distinguishing factor between fraud and error is the materiality of the transaction involved.
   B. An auditor who initially detects fraud ultimately makes the legal determination of whether fraud has actually occurred.
   C. Fraudulent financial reporting can include the unintentional misstatement of amounts or disclosures in financial statements.
   D. It is often difficult to detect fraudulent intent in matters involving accounting estimates and the application of accounting principles.

Fraud: Evaluation and Communication

AICPA.aq.Fraud.eval.001_17

167. During the course of an audit, an auditor finds evidence that an officer has entered fraudulent transactions in the financial statements. The fraudulent transactions can be adjusted so the statements are not materially misstated. What should the auditor do?

   A. Report the matters to regulatory authorities.
   B. Consider the fraud a scope limitation and disclaim an opinion.
   C. Communicate the matter to those charged with governance.
   D. Immediately withdraw from the engagement.

AICPA.aq.Fraud.eval.002_17

168. During an audit, an auditor discovers a fraudulent expense reimbursement for a low-level manager. The auditor determines that this transaction is inconsequential and several similar transactions would not be material to the financial statements in the aggregate. Which of the following statements **best** describes the auditor's required response to the discovery?

   A. The auditor should fully investigate other transactions related to this manager to determine if fraud exists.
   B. The auditor should bring the transaction to the attention of an appropriate level of management.
   C. The auditor should report this finding to those charged with governance.
   D. The auditor's responsibility is satisfied by documenting that the single transaction is inconsequential.

AICPA.900555AUD-AU

169. Disclosure of irregularities to parties other than a client's senior management and its audit committee or board of directors ordinarily is not part of an auditor's responsibility.

However, to which of the following outside parties may a duty to disclose irregularities exist?

	To the SEC When the Client Reports an Auditor Change	To a Successor Auditor When the Successor Makes Appropriate Inquiries	To a Government Funding Agency from Which the Client Receives Financial Assistance
A.	Yes	Yes	No
B.	Yes	No	Yes
C.	No	Yes	Yes
D.	Yes	Yes	Yes

Detecting Illegal Acts

AICPA.aq.det.illegal.001_18

170. Regarding a nonissuer's compliance with laws and regulations, an auditor performing an audit of the entity's financial statements is responsible for

A. Obtaining a general understanding of the legal and regulatory framework applicable to the entity and how the entity is complying with that framework.
B. Preventing noncompliance with existing applicable laws and regulations that determine reported amounts and disclosures in the entity's financial statements.
C. Determining whether an act performed by the entity being audited constitutes noncompliance with existing applicable laws and regulations.
D. Ensuring that the entity's operations are conducted in accordance with the provisions of laws and regulations relevant to the entity's financial statements.

AICPA.101093AUD

171. During the audit of a new client, the auditor determined that management had given illegal bribes to municipal officials during the year under audit and for several prior years. The auditor notified the client's board of directors, but the board decided to take no action because the amounts involved were immaterial to the financial statements. Under these circumstances, the auditor should

A. Add an explanatory paragraph emphasizing that certain matters, while not affecting the unqualified opinion, require disclosure.
B. Report the illegal bribes to the municipal official at least one level above those persons who received the bribes.
C. Consider withdrawing from the audit engagement and disassociating from future relationships with the client.
D. Issue an "except for" qualified opinion or an adverse opinion with a separate paragraph that explains the circumstances.

AICPA.101118AUD

172. Which of the following information that comes to an auditor's attention would be *most likely* to raise a question about the occurrence of illegal acts?

A. The exchange of property for similar property in a nonmonetary transaction.
B. The discovery of unexplained payments made to government employees.
C. The presence of several difficult-to-audit transactions affecting expense accounts.
D. The failure to develop adequate procedures that detect unauthorized purchases.

AICPA.970513AUD-AU

173. Which of the following information discovered during an audit *most likely* would raise a question concerning possible illegal acts?

A. Related party transactions, although properly disclosed, were pervasive during the year.
B. The entity prepared several large checks payable to cash during the year.
C. Material internal control weaknesses previously reported to management were not corrected.
D. The entity was a campaign contributor to several local political candidates during the year.

Using the Work of a Specialist

AICPA.aq.specialist.001_17

174. Under which of the following circumstances would an auditor be considered to be using the work of a specialist?

A. The auditor engages a lawyer to interpret the provisions of a complex contract.
B. The auditor makes inquiries of the client's lawyer regarding pending litigation.
C. A tax expert employed by the auditor's CPA firm reviews the client's tax accruals.
D. The client engages an outside computer service organization to prepare its payroll.

AICPA.070614AUD

175. An auditor intends to use the work of an actuary who has a relationship with the client. Under these circumstances, the auditor

A. Is required to disclose the contractual relationship in the auditor's report.
B. Should assess the risk that the actuary's objectivity might be impaired.
C. Is not permitted to rely on the actuary because of a lack of independence.
D. Should communicate this matter to the audit committee as a significant deficiency.

AICPA.090751.AUD.AU

176. Which of the following statements is correct concerning an auditor's use of the work of an actuary in assessing a client's pension obligations?

A. The auditor is required to understand the objectives and scope of the actuary's work.
B. The reasonableness of the actuary's assumptions is strictly the auditor's responsibility.
C. The client is required to consent to the auditor's use of the actuary's work.
D. If the actuary has a relationship with the client, the auditor may not use the actuary's work.

AICPA.090795.AUD-AU

177. An auditor who uses the work of a specialist may refer to the specialist in the auditor's report if the

A. Auditor believes that the specialist's findings are reasonable in the circumstances.
B. Specialist's findings support the related assertions in the financial statements.
C. Auditor modifies the report because of the difference between the client's and the specialist's valuations of an asset.
D. Specialist's findings provide the auditor with greater assurance of reliability about management's representations.

AICPA.941165AUD-AU

178. Which of the following statements is correct about the auditor's use of the work of a specialist?

A. The specialist should not have an understanding of the auditor's corroborative use of the specialist's findings.
B. The auditor is required to perform substantive procedures to verify the specialist's assumptions and findings.

C. The client should not have an understanding of the nature of the work to be performed by the specialist.
D. The auditor should obtain an understanding of the methods and assumptions used by the specialist.

Required Communications with those Charged with Governance

AICPA.aq.req.comm.001_18

179. During planning, an auditor of a nonissuer should communicate which of the following to those charged with governance at an entity?

A. The auditor is responsible for preparing financial statements in conformity with the applicable financial reporting framework.
B. The audit does not relieve management of its responsibilities for the financial statements.
C. The auditor will express an opinion on the effectiveness of internal controls over compliance with laws and regulations.
D. All audit findings will be communicated in writing to those charged with governance.

AICPA.931160AUD-AU

180. An auditor is obligated to communicate an uncorrected audit adjustment to an entity's audit committee (or those charged with governance) only if the adjustment

A. Is individually material.
B. Is not believed to be trivial.
C. Is a recurring matter that was proposed to management the prior year.
D. Results from the correction of a prior period's departure from GAAP.

AICPA.950519AUD-AU

181. An auditor would be *least likely* to initiate a discussion with a client's audit committee concerning

A. The methods used to account for significant unusual transactions.
B. The maximum dollar amount of misstatements that could exist without causing the financial statements to be materially misstated.
C. Indications of fraud and illegal acts committed by a corporate officer that were discovered by the auditor.
D. Disagreements with management as to accounting principles that were resolved during the current year's audit.

AICPA.950588AUD-AU

182. Which of the following statements is correct concerning an auditor's required communication with an entity's audit committee (or those charged with governance)?

A. This communication is required to occur before the auditor's report on the financial statements is issued.

B. This communication should include management changes in the application of significant accounting policies.

C. Any significant matter communicated to the audit committee (or those charged with governance) also should be communicated to management.

D. Significant audit adjustments proposed by the auditor and recorded by management need not be communicated to the audit committee (or those charged with governance.)

AICPA.951184AUD-AU

183. Which of the following statements is correct about an auditor's required communication with an entity's audit committee (or those charged with governance)?

A. Any matters communicated to the entity's audit committee (or those charged with governance) also are required to be communicated to the entity's management.

B. The auditor is required to inform the entity's audit committee (or those charged with governance) about errors discovered by the auditor and subsequently corrected by management.

C. Disagreements with management about the application of significant accounting principles are required to be communicated to the entity's audit committee (or those charged with governance).

D. All deficiencies or weaknesses in the internal control structure are required to be communicated to the audit committee.

AICPA.990427AUD-AU

184. During the planning phase of an audit, an auditor is identifying matters for communication to the entity's audit committee (or those charged with governance).

The auditor *most likely* would ask management whether

A. There was significant turnover in the accounting department.

B. It consulted with another CPA firm about installing a new computer system.

C. There were changes in the application of significant accounting policies.

D. It agreed with the auditor's selection of fraud detection procedures.

PCAOB on Communications with Audit Committees

AICPA.aq.pcaob.comm.aud.001_17

185. Which of the following groups is considered a subgroup ordinarily charged with assisting the board of directors in fulfilling its oversight responsibilities?

A. Audit committee.

B. Secured creditors.

C. Internal auditors.

D. Senior management.

AICPA.130503AUD-SIM

186. The objectives of Auditing Standard No. 16, "Communications with Audit Committees," include all of the following, except for

A. Enhancing communications between the audit committee and the entity's internal audit function.

B. Obtaining information from the audit committee that is relevant to the audit.

C. Providing the audit committee with timely information about significant audit issues.

D. Communicating to the audit committee the auditor's responsibilities and establish an understanding of the terms of the engagement.

AICPA.130504AUD-SIM

187. Under PCAOB auditing standards, the auditor should communicate all of the following matters to an issuer's audit committee at the beginning of the audit engagement except for

A. Significant issues that the auditor discussed with management in connection with the auditor's appointment/retention.

B. The terms of the engagement, including the objectives of the audit and the parties' respective responsibilities.

C. The qualitative aspects of the entity's significant accounting policies, including any indications of management bias.

D. An overview of the audit strategy and timing of the audit, along with any significant risks identified by the auditor.

AICPA.130505AUD-SIM

188. The format and timing of the auditor's required communication with an issuer's audit committee is best characterized by the following:

	Format of the Communication	Timing of the Communication
A.	Must be in writing	Must be by the date of the auditor's report
B.	Must be in writing	Must be prior to issuing the auditor's report
C.	May be written or oral (unless otherwise specified)	Must be by the date of the auditor's report
D.	May be written or oral (unless otherwise specified)	Must be prior to issuing the auditor's report

Internal Control—Concepts and Standards

Obtaining an Understanding of Internal Control

AICPA.120707AUD

189. Obtaining an understanding of an internal control involves evaluating the design of the control and determining whether the control has been

   A. Authorized.
   B. Implemented.
   C. Tested.
   D. Monitored.

AICPA.901143AUD-AU

190. An auditor's primary consideration regarding an entity's internal control structure policies and procedures is whether they

   A. Prevent management override.
   B. Relate to the control environment.
   C. Reflect management's philosophy and operating style.
   D. Affect the financial statement assertions.

AICPA.901144AUD-AU

191. In planning an audit of certain accounts, an auditor may conclude that specific procedures used to obtain an understanding of an entity's internal control structure need not be included because of the auditor's judgments about materiality and assessments of

   A. Control risk.
   B. Detection risk.
   C. Sampling risk.
   D. Inherent risk.

AICPA.920555AUD-AU

192. Decision tables differ from program flowcharts in that decision tables emphasize

   A. Ease of manageability for complex programs.
   B. Logical relationships among conditions and actions.
   C. Cost benefit factors justifying the program.
   D. The sequence in which operations are performed.

AICPA.951106AUD-AU

193. Which of the following is a management control method that *most likely* could improve management's ability to supervise company activities effectively?

   A. Monitoring compliance with internal control requirements imposed by regulatory bodies.
   B. Limiting direct access to assets by physical segregation and protective devices.
   C. Establishing budgets and forecasts to identify variances from expectations.
   D. Supporting employees with the resources necessary to discharge their responsibilities.

Evaluating Internal Control

AICPA.020406AUD-AU

194. When assessing control risk at below the maximum level, an auditor is required to document the auditor's understanding of the

   I. Entity's control activities that help ensure management directives are carried out.
   II. Entity's control environment factors that help the auditor plan the engagement.

   A. I only.
   B. II only.
   C. Both I and II.
   D. Neither I nor II.

AICPA.950527AUD-AU

195. Control risk should be assessed in terms of

    A. Specific control procedures.
    B. Types of potential irregularities.
    C. Financial statement assertions.
    D. Control environment factors.

AICPA.950533AUD-AU

196. After obtaining an understanding of the internal control structure and assessing control risk, an auditor decided to perform tests of controls. The auditor *most likely* decided that

    A. It would be efficient to perform tests of controls that would result in a reduction in planned substantive tests.
    B. Additional evidence to support a further reduction in control risk is not available.
    C. An increase in the assessed level of control risk is justified for certain financial statement assertions.
    D. There were many internal control structure weaknesses that could allow errors to enter the accounting system.

AICPA.951104AUD-AU

197. Which of the following auditor concerns could *most likely* be so serious that the auditor concludes that a financial statement audit cannot be conducted?

    A. The entity has no formal written code of conduct.
    B. The integrity of the entity's management is suspect.
    C. Procedures requiring segregation of duties are subject to management override.
    D. Management fails to modify prescribed controls for changes in conditions.

AICPA.951120AUD-AU

198. Which of the following statements is correct concerning an auditor's assessment of control risk?

    A. Assessing control risk may be performed concurrently during an audit with obtaining an understanding of the entity's internal control structure.
    B. Evidence about the operation of control procedures in prior audits may not be considered during the current year's assessment of control risk.
    C. The basis for an auditor's conclusions about the assessed level of control risk need not be documented unless control risk is assessed at the maximum level.

    D. The lower the assessed level of control risk, the less assurance the evidence must provide that the control procedures are operating effectively.

AICPA.951122AUD-AU

199. Assessing control risk at below the maximum level *most likely* would involve

    A. Performing more extensive substantive tests with larger sample sizes than originally planned.
    B. Reducing inherent risk for most of the assertions relevant to significant account balances.
    C. Changing the timing of substantive tests by omitting interim-date testing and performing the tests at year end.
    D. Identifying specific internal control structure policies and procedures relevant to specific assertions.

AICPA.951123AUD-AU

200. After assessing control risk at below the maximum level, an auditor desires to seek a further reduction in the assessed level of control risk. At this time, the auditor would consider whether

    A. It would be efficient to obtain an understanding of the entity's accounting system.
    B. The entity's internal control structure polices and procedures have been placed in operation.
    C. The entity's internal control structure polices and procedures pertain to any financial statement assertions.
    D. Additional evidential matter sufficient to support a further reduction is likely to be available.

Assessing Control Risk Under AICPA Standards

AICPA.020506AUD-AU

201. When assessing control risk at below the maximum level, an auditor is required to document the auditor's understanding of the

    I. Entity's control activities that help ensure management directives are carried out.
    II. Entity's control environment factors that help the auditor plan the engagement.

    A. I only.
    B. II only.
    C. Both I and II.
    D. Neither I nor II.

AICPA.090758.AUD.AU

202. Which of the following actions should the auditor take in response to discovering a deviation from the prescribed control procedure?

A. Make inquiries to understand the potential consequence of the deviation.
B. Assume that the deviation is an isolated occurrence without audit significance.
C. Report the matter to the next higher level of authority within the entity.
D. Increase sample size of tests of controls.

AICPA.111177AUD

203. Which of the following is not a component of internal control?

A. Control environment.
B. Control activities.
C. Inherent risk.
D. Monitoring.

AICPA.120710AUD

204. Which of the following is the best way to compensate for the lack of adequate segregation of duties in a small organization?

A. Disclosing lack of segregation of duties to the external auditors during the annual review.
B. Replacing personnel every three or four years.
C. Requiring accountants to pass a yearly background check.
D. Allowing for greater management oversight of incompatible activities.

AICPA.950526AUD-AU

205. When considering the internal control structure, an auditor should be aware of the concept of reasonable assurance, which recognizes that

A. Internal control policies and procedures may be ineffective due to mistakes in judgment and personal carelessness.
B. Adequate safeguards over access to assets and records should permit an entity to maintain proper accountability.
C. Establishing and maintaining the internal control structure is an important responsibility of management.
D. The cost of an entity's internal control structure should not exceed the benefits expected to be derived.

AICPA.951113AUD-AU

206. In obtaining an understanding of an entity's internal control structure policies and procedures that are relevant to audit planning, an auditor is required to obtain knowledge about the

A. Design of the policies and procedures pertaining to the internal control structure elements.
B. Effectiveness of the policies and procedures that have been placed in operation.
C. Consistency with which the policies and procedures are currently being applied.
D. Control procedures related to each principal transaction class and account balance.

Performing Procedures in Response to Assessed Risks

AICPA.020409AUD-AU

207. Which of the following auditor concerns *most likely* could be so serious that the auditor concludes that a financial statement audit cannot be performed?

A. Management fails to modify prescribed internal controls for changes in information technology.
B. Internal control activities requiring segregation of duties are rarely monitored by management.
C. Management is dominated by one person who is also the majority stockholder.
D. There is a substantial risk of intentional misapplication of accounting principles.

AICPA.070604AUD

208. When companies use information technology (IT) extensively, evidence may be available only in electronic form. What is an auditor's best course of action in such situations?

A. Assess the control risk as high.
B. Use audit software to perform analytical procedures.
C. Use generalized audit software to extract evidence from client databases.
D. Perform limited tests of controls over electronic data.

AICPA.130709AUD

209. When the operating effectiveness of a control is **not** evidenced by written documentation, an auditor should obtain evidence about the control's effectiveness by

A. Mailing confirmations.
B. Inquiry and other procedures such as observation.

C. Analytical procedures.

D. Recalculating the balance in related accounts.

AICPA.931121AUD-AU

210. An auditor may decide to assess control risk at the maximum level for certain assertions because the auditor believes

A. Control policies and procedures are unlikely to pertain to the assertions.

B. The entity's control environment, accounting system, and control procedures are interrelated.

C. Sufficient evidential matter to support the assertions is likely to be available.

D. More emphasis on tests of controls than substantive tests is warranted.

AICPA.941142AUD-AU

211. The objective of tests of details of transactions performed as tests of controls is to

A. Monitor the design and use of entity documents such as prenumbered shipping forms.

B. Determine whether internal control structure policies and procedures have been placed in operation.

C. Detect material misstatements in the account balances of the financial statements.

D. Evaluate whether internal control structure procedures operated effectively.

Required Communications

AICPA.010414AUD-AU

212. Which of the following matters would an auditor *most likely* consider to be a significant deficiency to be communicated to the audit committee (or otherwise those charged with governance)?

A. Management's failure to renegotiate unfavorable long-term purchase commitments.

B. Recurring operating losses that may indicate going concern problems.

C. Evidence of a lack of objectivity by those responsible for accounting decisions.

D. Management's current plans to reduce its ownership equity in the entity.

AICPA.020415AUD-AU

213. Which of the following factors should an auditor consider in making a judgment about whether an internal control deficiency is so significant that it is a significant deficiency?

I. Diversity of the entity's business.

II. Size of the entity's operations.

A. I only.

B. II only.

C. Both I and II.

D. Neither I nor II.

AICPA.941144AUD-AU

214. Significant deficiencies are matters that come to an auditor's attention that should be communicated to an entity's audit committee (or those charged with governance) because they represent

A. Disclosures of information that significantly contradict the auditor's going concern assumption.

B. Material irregularities or illegal acts perpetrated by high-level management.

C. Significant deficiencies in the design or operation of internal control.

D. Manipulation or falsification of accounting records or documents from which financial statements are prepared.

assess.AICPA.AUD.ic.req.comm-0015

215. To what degree, if at all, is a significant deficiency related to a material weakness?

A. It is **less** severe than a material weakness.

B. It is more severe than a material weakness.

C. It is unrelated to a material weakness.

D. It is equivalent to a material weakness.

assess.AICPA.AUD.ic.req.comm-0018

216. The auditor is required to communicate each of the following items to those charged with governance **except**

A. An overview of the planned scope and timing of the audit.

B. The auditor's responsibilities to complete the audit in accordance with generally accepted auditing standards.

C. All control deficiencies detected during the course of the audit.

D. Any significant findings from the audit.

assess.AICPA.AUD.req.comm-0021

217. Which of the following matters in a financial statement audit is most appropriate to communicate with those charged with governance?

A. Clearance explanations of workpaper review notes.

B. Major variances in budgeted versus actual audit hours

C. The nature and timing of detailed audit procedures

D. An overview of the planned scope and timing of the audit

Using the Work of an Internal Audit Function

AICPA.020518AUD-AU

218. In assessing the objectivity of internal auditors, the independent CPA who is auditing the entity's financial statements would *most likely* consider the

A. Internal auditing standards developed by The Institute of Internal Auditors.

B. Tests of internal control activities that could detect errors and fraud.

C. Materiality of the accounts recently inspected by the internal auditors.

D. Results of the tests of transactions recently performed by the internal auditors.

AICPA.090791.AUD-AU

219. When assessing the competence of the internal auditors, an independent CPA should obtain information about the

A. Organizational level to which the internal auditors report.

B. Quality of the internal auditors' working paper documentation.

C. Policies prohibiting internal auditors from auditing sensitive matters.

D. Internal auditors' preliminary assessed level of control risk.

AICPA.111189AUD

220. When assessing internal auditors' objectivity, an independent auditor should

A. Consider the policies that prohibit the internal auditors from auditing areas where they were recently assigned.

B. Review the internal auditors' reports to determine that their conclusions are consistent with the work performed.

C. Verify that the internal auditors' assessment of control risk is comparable to the independent auditor's assessment.

D. Evaluate the quality of the internal auditors' working paper documentation and their recent audit recommendations.

AICPA.130706AUD

221. Which of the following factors should an external auditor obtain updated information about when assessing an internal auditor's competence?

A. The reporting status of the internal auditor within the organization.

B. The educational level and professional experiences of the internal auditor.

C. Whether policies prohibit the internal auditor from auditing areas where relatives are employed.

D. Whether the board of directors, audit committee, or owner-manager oversees employment decisions related to the internal auditor.

AICPA.951153AUD-AU

222. The work of internal auditors may affect the independent auditor's

I. Procedures performed in obtaining an understanding of the internal control structure.

II. Procedures performed in assessing the risk of material misstatement.

III. Substantive procedures performed in gathering direct evidence.

A. I and II only.

B. I and III only.

C. II and III only.

D. I, II, and III.

assess.AICPA.AUD.internal.aud-0031

223. An entity has an internal audit staff that the independent auditor assessed to be both competent and objective. Which of the following statements is correct about the independent auditor's use of the internal auditors to provide direct assistance in performing tests of controls?

A. The auditor **cannot** rely on any of the work of the internal auditors.

B. The internal auditors should **not** be performing any audit procedures that the auditor is able to perform.

C. The auditor can use internal auditors to assess control risk but **cannot** rely on their tests of controls.

D. The auditor should supervise, review, evaluate, and test the work performed by the internal auditors.

Performing Further Procedures and Obtaining Evidence

Internal Control: Transaction Cycles

Specific Transaction Cycles

AICPA.010504AUD-AU

224. An auditor suspects that certain client employees are ordering merchandise for themselves over the Internet without recording the purchase or receipt of the merchandise. When vendors' invoices arrive, one of the employees approves the invoices for payment. After the invoices are paid, the employee destroys the invoices and the related vouchers.

    In gathering evidence regarding the fraud, the auditor would *most likely* select items for testing from the file of all

    A. Cash disbursements.
    B. Approved vouchers.
    C. Receiving reports.
    D. Vendors' invoices.

AICPA.941126AUD-AU

225. Proper segregation of duties reduces the opportunities to allow persons to be in positions to both

    A. Journalize entries and prepare financial statements.
    B. Record cash receipts and cash disbursements.
    C. Establish internal controls and authorize transactions.
    D. Perpetrate and conceal errors and irregularities.

Revenue/Receipts—Sales

AICPA.aq.rev.sales.001_17

226. Which of the following could indicate source document fraud?

    A. The same customer purchase order number appears on different customer invoices.
    B. The same item code appears on different invoices.
    C. The same invoice number appears on different invoices.
    D. The same invoice date appears on different invoices.

AICPA.090787.AUD-AU

227. An auditor's tests of controls for completeness for the revenue cycle usually include determining whether

    A. Each receivable is collected subsequent to the year-end.
    B. An invoice is prepared for each shipping document.
    C. Each invoice is supported by a customer purchase order.
    D. Each credit memo is properly approved.

AICPA.941135AUD-AU

228. Proper authorization of write-offs of uncollectible accounts should be approved in which of the following departments?

    A. Accounts receivable.
    B. Credit.
    C. Accounts payable.
    D. Treasurer.

AICPA.970414AUD-AU

229. Which of the following fraudulent activities could *most likely* be perpetrated due to the lack of effective internal controls in the revenue cycle?

    A. Fictitious transactions may be recorded that cause an understatement of revenues and an overstatement of receivables.
    B. Claims received from customers for goods returned may be intentionally recorded in other customers' accounts.
    C. Authorization of credit memos by personnel who receive cash may permit the misappropriation of cash.
    D. The failure to prepare shipping documents may cause an overstatement of inventory balances.

Revenue/Receipts—Cash

AICPA.020507AUD-AU

230. Which of the following circumstances would *most likely* cause an auditor to suspect that material misstatements exist in a client's financial statements?

A. The assumptions used in developing the prior year's accounting estimates have changed.
B. Differences between reconciliations of control accounts and subsidiary records are not investigated.
C. Negative confirmation requests yield fewer responses than in the prior year's audit.
D. Management consults with another CPA firm about complex accounting matters.

AICPA.950530AUD-AU

231. Sound internal control procedures dictate that, immediately upon receiving checks from customers by mail, a responsible employee should

A. Add the checks to the daily cash summary.
B. Verify that each check is supported by a prenumbered sales invoice.
C. Prepare a duplicate listing of checks received.
D. Record the checks in the cash receipts journal.

AICPA.951112AUD-AU

232. Which of the following internal controls would be *most likely* to reduce the risk of diversion of customer receipts by an entity's employees?

A. A bank lockbox system.
B. Prenumbered remittance advices.
C. Monthly bank reconciliations.
D. Daily deposit of cash receipts.

AICPA.951146AUD-AU

233. An auditor would be *most likely* to limit substantive audit tests of sales transactions when control risk is assessed as low for the existence or occurrence assertion concerning sales transactions and the auditor has already gathered evidence supporting

A. Opening and closing inventory balances.
B. Cash receipts and accounts receivable.
C. Shipping and receiving activities.
D. Cutoffs of sales and purchases.

Expenditures/Disbursements

AICPA.090755.AUD.AU

234. Which of the following situations could *most likely* lead to an embezzlement scheme?

A. The accounts receivable bookkeeper receives a list of payments prepared by the cashier and personally makes entries in the customers' accounts receivable subsidiary ledger.
B. Each vendor invoice is matched with the related purchase order and receiving report by the vouchers payable bookkeeper who personally approves the voucher for payment.
C. Access to blank checks and signature plates is restricted to the cash disbursements bookkeeper who personally reconciles the monthly bank statement.
D. Vouchers and supporting documentation are examined and then canceled by the treasurer who personally mails the checks to vendors.

AICPA.120727AUD

235. Which of the following controls should prevent an invoice for the purchase of merchandise from being paid twice?

A. The check signer accounts for the numerical sequence of receiving reports used in support of each payment.
B. An individual independent of cash operations prepares a bank reconciliation.
C. The check signer reviews and cancels the voucher packets.
D. Two check signers are required for all checks over a specified amount.

AICPA.940530AUD-AU

236. In a properly designed internal control structure, the same employee would *most likely* match vendors' invoices with receiving reports and also

A. Post the detailed accounts payable records.
B. Recompute the calculations on vendors' invoices.
C. Reconcile the accounts payable ledger.
D. Cancel vendors' invoices after payment.

AICPA.951129AUD-AU

237. In testing controls over cash disbursements, an auditor would be *most likely* to determine that the person who signs checks also

A. Reviews the monthly bank reconciliation.
B. Returns the checks to accounts payable.

C. Is denied access to the supporting documents.

D. Is responsible for mailing the checks.

Payroll Cycle

AICPA.101095AUD

238. Which of the following activities performed by a department supervisor would *most likely* help in the prevention or detection of a payroll fraud?

   A. Distributing paychecks directly to department employees.
   B. Setting the pay rate for departmental employees.
   C. Hiring employees and authorizing them to be added to payroll.
   D. Approving a summary of hours each employee worked during the pay period.

AICPA.101121AUD

239. Which of the following payroll control activities would most effectively ensure that payment is made only for work performed?

   A. Require all employees to record arrival and departure by using the time clock.
   B. Have a payroll clerk recalculate all time cards.
   C. Require all employees to sign their time cards.
   D. Require employees to have their direct supervisors approve their time cards.

Miscellaneous Cycles

AICPA.931128AUD-AU

240. The objectives of the internal control structure for a production cycle are to provide assurance that transactions are properly executed and recorded, and that

   A. Production orders are prenumbered and signed by a supervisor.
   B. Custody of work in process and of finished goods is properly maintained.
   C. Independent internal verification of activity reports is established.
   D. Transfers to finished goods are documented by a completed production report and a quality control report.

AICPA.931132AUD-AU

241. Which of the following questions would an auditor *most likely* include on an internal control questionnaire for notes payable?

   A. Are assets that collateralize notes payable critically needed for the entity's continued existence.
   B. Are two or more authorized signatures required on checks that repay notes payable?
   C. Are the proceeds from notes payable used for the purchase of noncurrent assets?
   D. Are direct borrowings on notes payable authorized by the board of directors?

AICPA.940532AUD-AU

242. Which of the following internal control procedures would *most likely* prevent direct labor hours from being charged to manufacturing overhead?

   A. Periodic independent counts of work in process for comparison to recorded amounts.
   B. Comparison of daily journal entries with approved production orders.
   C. Use of time tickets to record actual labor worked on production orders.
   D. Reconciliation of work-in-process inventory with periodic cost budgets.

AICPA.940534AUD-AU

243. When an entity uses a trust company as custodian of its marketable securities, the possibility of concealing fraud would *most likely* be reduced if the

   A. Trust company has no direct contact with the entity employees responsible for maintaining investment accounting records.
   B. Securities are registered in the name of the trust company, rather than the entity itself.
   C. Interest and dividend checks are mailed directly to an entity employee who is authorized to sell securities.
   D. Trust company places the securities in a bank safe-deposit vault under the custodian's exclusive control.

AICPA.951127AUD-AU

244. When there are numerous property and equipment transactions during the year, an auditor who plans to assess control risk at a low level usually performs

    A. Tests of controls and extensive tests of property and equipment balances at the end of the year.
    B. Analytical procedures for current year property and equipment transactions.
    C. Tests of controls and limited tests of current year property and equipment transactions.
    D. Analytical procedures for property and equipment balances at the end of the year.

Audit Evidence: Concepts and Standards

Overview of Substantive Procedures

AICPA.070643AUD

245. At the conclusion of an audit, an auditor is reviewing the evidence gathered in support of the financial statements. With regard to the valuation of inventory, the auditor concludes that the evidence obtained is not sufficient to support management's representations. Which of the following actions is the auditor *most likely* to take?

    A. Consult with the audit committee and issue a disclaimer of opinion.
    B. Consult with the audit committee and issue a qualified opinion.
    C. Obtain additional evidence regarding the valuation of inventory.
    D. Obtain a statement from management supporting their inventory valuation.

AICPA.090796.AUD-AU

246. Which of the following ratios would an engagement partner *most likely* consider in the overall review stage of an audit?

    A. Total liabilities/net sales.
    B. Accounts receivable/inventory.
    C. Cost of goods sold/average inventory.
    D. Current assets/quick assets.

AICPA.950501AUD-AU

247. The element of the audit planning process *most likely* to be agreed upon with the client before implementation of the audit strategy is the determination of the

    A. Evidence to be gathered to provide a sufficient basis for the auditor's opinion.
    B. Procedures to be undertaken to discover litigation, claims, and assessments.
    C. Pending legal matters to be included in the inquiry of the client's attorney.
    D. Timing of inventory observation procedures to be performed.

assess.AICPA.AUD.sub.proc-0029

248. Which of the following best identifies the effect of an increase in the risk of material misstatement on detection risk and the extent of substantive procedures?

    A. The acceptable level of detection risk decreases, and the extent of substantive procedures increases.
    B. The acceptable level of detection risk increases, and the extent of substantive procedures increases.
    C. The acceptable level of detection risk decreases, and the extent of substantive procedures decreases.
    D. The acceptable level of detection risk increases, and the extent of substantive procedures decreases.

assess.AICPA.AUD.sub.proc-0030

249. Which of the following is an analytical procedure?

    A. Comparing current-year balances to prior-year balances.
    B. Matching sales invoices to shipping documents.
    C. Confirming accounts receivable.
    D. Making inquiries of client management.

The Nature of Audit Evidence

AICPA.020411AUD-AU

250. An auditor observed that a client mails monthly statements to customers. Subsequently, the auditor reviewed evidence of follow-up on the errors reported by the customers.

This test of controls *most likely* was performed to support management's financial statement assertion(s) of

	Presentation and Disclosure	Rights and Obligations
A.	Yes	Yes
B.	Yes	No
C.	No	Yes
D.	No	No

AICPA.130731AUD

251. Which of the following is a management assertion regarding account balances at the period end?

   A. Transactions and events that have been recorded have occurred and pertain to the entity.
   B. Transactions and events have been recorded in the proper accounts.
   C. The entity holds or controls the rights to assets, and liabilities are obligations of the entity.
   D. Amounts and other data related to transactions and events have been recorded appropriately.

AICPA.950539AUD-AU

252. Which of the following types of audit evidence is the most persuasive?

   A. Prenumbered client purchase order forms.
   B. Client work sheets supporting cost allocations.
   C. Bank statements obtained from the client.
   D. Client representation letter.

assess.AICPA.AUD.evidence1-0027

253. Which of the following ultimately determines the sufficiency and appropriateness of audit evidence to support the auditor's conclusions?

   A. Professional requirements.
   B. Professional standards.
   C. Professional experience.
   D. Professional judgment.

assess.AICPA.AUD.evidence1-0028

254. Which of the following assertions is most closely related to the audit objective to verify that all sales have been recorded?

   A. Completeness.
   B. Occurrence.
   C. Accuracy.
   D. Cutoff.

Assertions and Types of Audit Procedures

AICPA.010512AUD-AU

255. Which of the following procedures would an auditor *most likely* perform during an audit engagement's overall review stage in formulating an opinion on an entity's financial statements?

   A. Obtain assurance from the entity's attorney that all material litigation has been disclosed in the financial statements.
   B. Verify the clerical accuracy of the entity's proof of cash and its bank cutoff statement.

   C. Determine whether inadequate provisions for the safeguarding of assets have been corrected.
   D. Consider whether the results of audit procedures affect the assessment of the risk of material misstatement due to fraud.

AICPA.070615AUD

256. Before applying principal substantive tests to an entity's accounts receivable at an interim date, an auditor should:

   A. Consider the likelihood of assessing the risk of incorrect rejection too low.
   B. Project sampling risk at the maximum for tests covering the remaining period.
   C. Ascertain that accounts receivable are immaterial to the financial statements.
   D. Assess the difficulty in controlling the incremental audit risk.

AICPA.101123AUD

257. Which of the following procedures is considered a test of controls?

   A. An auditor reviews the entity's check register for unrecorded liabilities.
   B. An auditor evaluates whether a general journal entry was recorded at the proper amount.
   C. An auditor interviews and observes appropriate personnel to determine segregation of duties.
   D. An auditor reviews the audit documentation to ensure proper sign-off.

AICPA.130713AUD

258. Which of the following is an important consideration when deciding the nature of tests to use in a financial statement audit?

   A. Tests of details typically provide a low level of assurance.
   B. Analytical procedures are an inefficient means of obtaining assurance.
   C. The procedures to be applied on a particular engagement are a matter of the auditor's professional judgment.
   D. The use of tests of controls should be considered without regard to the level of assurance required.

AICPA.130737AUD

259. An auditor of a nonissuer should design tests of details to ensure that sufficient audit evidence supports which of the following?

   A. The planned level of control risk.
   B. Management's assertions that internal controls exist and are operating efficiently.
   C. The effectiveness of internal controls.
   D. The planned level of assurance at the relevant assertion level.

assess.AICPA.AUD.evidence2-0037

260. If an auditor of an issuer examines purchase orders obtained from the issuer to verify proper authorization of transactions, then the auditor is conducting

   A. A reperformance.
   B. A confirmation.
   C. An observation.
   D. An inspection.

PCAOB Risk Assessment Standards

AICPA.111151AUD-SIM

261. The PCAOB identifies each of the following as a financial statement assertion to be addressed by the auditor except for

   A. Existence or occurrence.
   B. Completeness.
   C. Cutoff.
   D. Presentation and disclosure.

AICPA.111153AUD-SIM

262. In PCAOB AS Section 2110, *Identifying and Assessing Risks of Material Misstatement*, the PCAOB states that the auditor should perform all of the following as risk assessment procedures except for

   A. Incorporating a degree of unpredictability in planned audit procedures.
   B. Obtaining an understanding of the company and its environment.
   C. Performing analytical procedures.
   D. Inquiring of the audit committee, management, and others within the company about the risks of material misstatement.

AICPA.130718AUD

263. When a PCAOB auditing standard indicates that an auditor "could" perform a specific procedure, how should the auditor decide whether and how to perform the procedure?

   A. By comparing the PCAOB standard with related AICPA auditing standards.

   B. By exercising professional judgment in the circumstances.
   C. By soliciting input from the issuer's audit committee.
   D. By evaluating whether the audit is likely to be subject to inspection by the PCAOB.

Evaluation of Misstatements Identified During the Audit

AICPA.aq.eval.miss.001_17

264. Misstatements discovered by the auditor were immaterial in the aggregate in prior years. Such misstatements should be

   A. Considered in the evaluation of audit findings in the current year.
   B. Disclosed by the client in the current-year financial statements.
   C. Retested during the current-year tests of controls.
   D. Removed from the prior-year summary because they were immaterial.

AICPA.101135AUD-SIM

265. For all (non-trivial) factual misstatements identified by the auditor, the auditor should

   A. Request management to review their assumptions and methods used to develop a more appropriate accounting estimate.
   B. Communicate the matters to the appropriate level of management to request correction.
   C. Obtain an understanding of management's justification and modify the audit report to express an adverse opinion.
   D. Make the appropriate adjusting journal entries to correct the identified misstatements.

AICPA.130511AUD-SIM

266. An auditor is not required to document

   A. Identified material misstatements that have been corrected by management.
   B. The basis for the auditor's determination of materiality levels used.
   C. Senior management's awareness of (and agreement with) the tolerable misstatement specified by the auditor for material elements of the financial statements.
   D. The auditor's conclusion as to whether any misstatements that management chose not to correct are, in fact, material.

AICPA.130512AUD-SIM

267. The term *judgmental misstatement* would best apply to

   A. Management's unreasonable accounting estimates for uncollectible receivables.
   B. Sales transactions that were recorded but not yet shipped as of year-end.
   C. Unrecorded payables associated with goods received in the last month of the entity's fiscal year.
   D. The auditor's estimate of a misstatement in a population suggested by audit sampling techniques.

assess.AICPA.AUD.eval.miss-0038

268. In a financial statement audit of a nonissuer, an auditor would consider a judgmental misstatement to be a misstatement that

   A. Involves an estimate.
   B. Exists because of nonstatistical sampling performed by the auditor.
   C. Arises from a flaw in the accounting system.
   D. Arises from a routine calculation.

Audit Documentation

AICPA.aq.aud.doc.proc.001_17

269. Which of the following statements is **correct** about actions taken after the documentation completion date?

   A. An auditor must **not** make any amendments to audit documentation before the end of the specified retention period.
   B. An auditor must **not** make any additions to audit documentation before the end of the specified retention period.
   C. An auditor must **not** make any changes to audit documentation before the end of the specified retention period.
   D. The auditor must **not** make any deletions to audit documentation before the end of the specified retention period.

AICPA.aq.aud.doc.proc.002_17

270. Which of the following statements is **most** accurate regarding audit documentation requirements?

   A. The auditor should document findings that could result in a modification of the auditor's report.
   B. If different audit procedures were performed due to a lack of responsiveness by the client, the lack of responsiveness should **not** be included in the working papers.

   C. If an oral explanation serves as sufficient support for the work the auditor performed, the explanation should be documented in the working papers.
   D. If the results of audit procedures indicate a need to revise the previous assessment of risk, the new assessment should be documented and the original assessment should be removed.

AICPA.941117AUD-AU

271. The permanent file of an auditor's documentation generally would not include

   A. Bond indenture agreements.
   B. Lease agreements.
   C. Working trial balance.
   D. Flowchart of internal control structure.

AICPA.950570AUD-AU

272. Which of the following pairs of accounts would an auditor *most likely* analyze on the same audit documentation?

   A. Notes receivable and interest income.
   B. Accrued interest receivable and accrued interest payable.
   C. Notes payable and notes receivable.
   D. Interest income and interest expense.

AICPA.950571AUD-AU

273. An auditor's documentation serves mainly to

   A. Provide the principal support for the auditor's report.
   B. Satisfy the auditor's responsibilities concerning the Code of Professional Conduct.
   C. Monitor the effectiveness of the CPA firm's quality control procedures.
   D. Document the level of independence maintained by the auditor.

PCAOB on Audit Documentation

AICPA08115001.AUD.SOA.3

274. Audit documentation associated with public companies must be retained for at least

   A. 3 years.
   B. 5 years.
   C. 7 years.
   D. 10 years.

AICPA08115001.AUD.SOA.4

275. For audits of public companies, audit documentation must be assembled within how many days of the report release date?

   A. 30 days.
   B. 45 days.
   C. 60 days.
   D. 90 days.

AICPA08115001.AUD.SOA.5

276. According to PCAOB auditing standards, after the documentation completion date,

   A. Documentation can be added or deleted as deemed appropriate.
   B. Documentation can be added but not deleted.
   C. Documentation cannot be added but can be deleted.
   D. Documentation cannot be added or deleted.

Confirmation

AICPA.090742.AUD.AU

277. The blank form of accounts receivable confirmations may be less efficient than the positive form because

   A. Shipping documents need to be inspected.
   B. Recipients may sign the forms without proper investigation.
   C. More nonresponses to the requests are likely to occur.
   D. Subsequent cash receipts need to be verified.

AICPA.120714AUD

278. Under which of the following circumstances should an auditor consider confirming the terms of a large complex sale?

   A. When the assessed level of control risk over the sale is low.
   B. When the assessed level of detection risk over the sale is high.
   C. When the combined assessed level of inherent and control risk over the sale is moderate.
   D. When the combined assessed level of inherent and control risk over the sale is high.

AICPA.950545AUD-AU

279. Which of the following statements is correct concerning the use of negative confirmation requests?

   A. Unreturned negative confirmation requests rarely provide significant explicit evidence.
   B. Negative confirmation requests are effective when detection risk is low.
   C. Unreturned negative confirmation requests indicate that alternative procedures are necessary.
   D. Negative confirmation requests are effective when understatements of account balances are suspected.

AICPA.970518AUD-AU

280. To reduce the risks associated with accepting fax responses to requests for confirmations of accounts receivable, an auditor *most likely* would

   A. Examine the shipping documents that provide evidence for the existence assertion.
   B. Verify the sources and contents of the faxes in telephone calls to the senders.
   C. Consider the faxes to be nonresponses and evaluate them as unadjusted differences.
   D. Inspect the faxes for forgeries or alterations and consider them to be acceptable if none are noted.

AICPA.980523AUD-AU

281. Under which of the following circumstances would the use of the blank form of confirmations of accounts receivable *most likely* be preferable to positive confirmations?

   A. The recipients are likely to sign the confirmations without devoting proper attention to them.
   B. Subsequent cash receipts are unusually difficult to verify.
   C. Analytical procedures indicate that few exceptions are expected.
   D. The combined assessed level of inherent risk and control risk is low.

Accounting Estimates

AICPA.020404AUD-AU

282. Which of the following procedures *most likely* would assist an auditor in determining whether management has identified all accounting estimates that could be material to the financial statements?

   A. Inquire about the existence of related party transactions.
   B. Determine whether accounting estimates deviate from historical patterns.
   C. Confirm inventories at locations outside the entity.
   D. Review the lawyer's letter for information about litigation.

AICPA.090314AUD-SIM

283. In evaluating the reasonableness of an entity's accounting estimates, an auditor normally would be concerned about assumptions that are

   A. Susceptible to bias.
   B. Consistent with prior periods.
   C. Insensitive to variations.
   D. Similar to industry guidelines.

AICPA.090747.AUD.AU

284. Which of the following statements is correct regarding accounting estimates?

   A. The auditor's objective is to evaluate whether accounting estimates are reasonable in the circumstances.
   B. Accounting estimates should be used when data concerning past events can be accumulated in a timely, cost-effective manner.
   C. An important accounting estimate is management's listing of accounts receivable greater than 90 days past due.
   D. Accounting estimates should not be used when the outcome of future events related to the estimated item is unknown.

assess.AICPA.AUD.act.est-0013

285. Which of the following audit procedures would be most appropriate to test the valuation of the collateral of a delinquent loan receivable?

   A. Sending a positive confirmation letter to the debtor to confirm the loan balance.
   B. Performing a site visit to physically inspect the collateral.
   C. Reviewing the debtor's purchase records to test the historical value of the collateral.
   D. Obtaining a current value appraisal of the collateral.

Fair Value Estimates

AICPA.aq.fv.est.001_17

286. An auditor is assessing the appropriateness of management's rationale for selecting a model to measure the fair value of debt securities. If, during the current year, an active trading market for the debt security was introduced, the auditor should validate each of the following criteria, **except** whether the valuation model is

   A. Appropriate for the environment in which the entity operates.
   B. Consistently applied from prior periods.
   C. Evaluated and appropriately applied based on generally accepted accounting principles.
   D. Appropriate for the debt security being valued.

AICPA.101141AUD

287. The auditor's responsibility to communicate with those charged with governance about fair value measurements and disclosure issues is best described by the following statement:

   A. The auditor should determine whether those charged with governance are informed about management's processes in developing material fair value estimates, including significant assumptions used by management.
   B. The auditor should determine whether those charged with governance are actively involved in designing and taking responsibility for the adequacy of internal controls over fair value measurements and disclosures.
   C. The auditor should determine whether those charged with governance were consulted by management and had adequate input in forming the entity's estimates for fair value measurement and disclosures.
   D. The auditor should determine whether those charged with governance take responsibility for the reasonableness of the entity's fair value measurements and disclosures.

AICPA.101142AUD

288. Which of the following statements describing the auditor's responsibilities when evaluating an entity's fair value measurements and disclosures is *incorrect*?

   A. The auditor is responsible for obtaining an understanding of relevant controls related to fair value measurement and disclosures.
   B. The auditor is responsible for determining that the entity's fair value measurements and methods used meet the requirements of GAAP and are consistently applied.
   C. The auditor is responsible for engaging a specialist to evaluate the reasonableness of the fair value measurements and disclosures whenever those fair value measurements are material to an entity's financial statements.
   D. The auditor is responsible for obtaining sufficient appropriate evidence to provide reasonable assurance that fair value measurements and disclosures meet the requirements of GAAP.

AICPA.101143AUD

289. When there are no observable market prices, the auditor is not obligated to consider whether

A. Management's valuation method is appropriate in the circumstances.
B. Management's selection of a specialist is appropriate for the audit engagement.
C. Management's valuation method is appropriate relative to the industry and environment of the entity.
D. Management has appropriately applied criteria provided by GAAP.

Lawyer's Letters

AICPA.090789.AUD-AU

290. Which of the following procedures would be *most likely* to assist an auditor in identifying litigation, claims, and assessments?

A. Inspect checks included with the client's cut-off bank statement.
B. Obtain a letter of representations from the client's underwriter of securities.
C. Apply ratio analysis on the current-year's liability accounts.
D. Read the file of correspondence from taxing authorities.

AICPA.101129AUD

291. What is an auditor's primary method to corroborate information on litigation, claims, and assessments?

A. Examining legal invoices sent by the client's attorney.
B. Verifying attorney-client privilege through interviews.
C. Reviewing the response from the client's lawyer to a letter of audit inquiry.
D. Reviewing the written representation letter obtained from management.

AICPA.111165AUD

292. Which of the following statements, extracted from a client's lawyer's letter concerning litigation, claims, and assessments, would be *most likely* to cause the auditor to request clarification?

A. "We believe that the possible liability to the company is nominal in amount."
B. "We believe that the action can be settled for less than the damages claimed."
C. "We believe that the plaintiff's case against the company is without merit."
D. "We believe that the company will be able to defend this action successfully."

AICPA.111191AUD

293. In auditing contingent liabilities, which of the following procedures would an auditor be *most likely* to perform?

A. Confirm the details of outstanding purchase orders.
B. Apply analytical procedures to accounts payable.
C. Read the minutes of the board of directors' meetings.
D. Perform tests of controls on the cash disbursement activities.

Management Representations Letters

AICPA.aq.mgmt.rep.001_17

294. Which of the following statements would an auditor *most likely* require management to indicate in a written representation letter obtained for an audit?

A. Management acknowledges its responsibilities for the design and implementation of programs and controls to detect fraud.
B. Management plans to expand into international operations during the next few years.
C. Management believes the financial statements are accurately stated in accordance with generally accepted auditing standards (GAAS).
D. Management believes the company is the premier company in its industry regarding service to customers.

AICPA.aq.mgmt.rep.002_17

295. Management's responses to inquiries can be corroborated by each of the following, **except**

A. Visits to the entity's premises and plant facilities.
B. Inspection of documents and internal control manuals.
C. Preparation of the summary of unadjusted differences.
D. Observation of entity activities and operations.

AICPA.101130AUD

296. Which of the following management roles would typically be acknowledged in a management representation letter?

A. Management has the responsibility for the design of controls to detect fraud.
B. Management communicates its views on ethical behavior to its employees.

C. Management's knowledge of fraud is communicated to the audit committee.

D. Management's compensation is contingent upon operating results.

AICPA.120715AUD

297. Of which of the following matters is a management representation letter required to contain specific representations?

A. Length of a material contract with a new customer.

B. Information concerning fraud by the CFO.

C. Reason for a significant increase in revenue over the prior year.

D. The competency and objectivity of the internal audit department.

AICPA.990526AUD-AU

298. Key Co. plans to present comparative financial statements for the years ended December 31, 2005, and 2006, respectively. Smith, CPA, audited Key's financial statements for both years and plans to report on the comparative financial statements on May 1, 2007. Key's current management team was not present until January 1, 2006. What period of time should be covered by Key's management representation letter?

A. January l, 2005, through December 31, 2006.

B. January 1, 2005, through May 1, 2007.

C. January 1, 2006, through December 31, 2006.

D. January 1, 2006, through May 1, 2007.

Related Party Issues

AICPA.aq.rel.party.001_17

299. What is the primary purpose of reviewing conflict-of-interest statements signed by members of management?

A. To obtain an understanding of business processes.

B. To identify transactions with related parties.

C. To assess control risk.

D. To consider limitations of internal control.

AICPA.120705AUD

300. In auditing related party transactions, an auditor ordinarily places primary emphasis on

A. The probability that related party transactions will recur.

B. Confirming the existence of the related parties.

C. Verifying the valuation of the related party transactions.

D. The adequacy of the disclosure of the related party transactions.

AICPA.920531AUD-AU

301. When auditing related party transactions, an auditor places primary emphasis on

A. Confirming the existence of the related parties.

B. Verifying the valuation of the related party transactions.

C. Evaluating the disclosure of the related party transactions.

D. Ascertaining the rights and obligations of the related parties.

AICPA.951158AUD-AU

302. Which of the following auditing procedures would be *most likely* to assist an auditor in identifying related party transactions?

A. Inspecting correspondence with lawyers for evidence of unreported contingent liabilities.

B. Vouching accounting records for recurring transactions recorded just after the balance sheet date.

C. Reviewing confirmations of loans receivable and payable for indications of guarantees.

D. Performing analytical procedures to seek indications of possible financial difficulties.

PCAOB on Related Parties

AICPA.151007AUD-SIM

303. PCAOB auditing standards dealing with related-party issues specifically require an auditor of an issuer to obtain an understanding of the company's process for each of the following except for

A. Identifying related parties and transactions with related parties.

B. Authorizing and approving transactions with related parties.

C. Determining that the terms of related-party transactions are substantially equivalent to those prevailing in arm's-length transactions with unrelated parties.

D. Accounting for and disclosing relationships and transactions with related parties in the financial statements.

AICPA.151009AUD-SIM

304. PCAOB auditing standards require an auditor of a public company to communicate with the audit committee about a variety of related-party matters. Each of the following is required to be communicated with the audit committee except

A. The auditor's evaluation of the company's identification and financial reporting treatment of related-party relationships and transactions.

B. Management's justification for engaging in transactions with a related party instead of arm's-length transactions with unrelated parties.

C. Related-party relationships or transactions with parties discovered by the auditor that were previously undisclosed to the auditor.

D. Related-party transactions identified by the auditor that appear to lack an appropriate business purpose.

AICPA.151010AUD-SIM

305. Suppose that management of an issuer makes an assertion in a footnote to the company's financial statements that material transactions with related parties were conducted on terms equivalent to those prevailing in arm's-length transactions. If evidence cannot be obtained to support this assertion and management declines to alter that footnote, what type of audit opinion would be appropriate?

A. Unqualified with an explanatory paragraph.

B. Qualified for a scope limitation.

C. Qualified or adverse for a material misstatement.

D. Disclaimer of opinion.

Subsequent Events and Related Issues

AICPA.aq.sub.events.001_17

306. Which of the following events that occurred after a client's calendar-year end, but before the audit report date, would require disclosure in the notes to the financial statements, but **no** adjustment in the financial statements?

A. New convertible bonds are issued to expand the company's product line.

B. A loss is reported on uncollectible accounts of an acknowledged distressed customer.

C. A fixed asset used in operations is sold at a substantial profit.

D. Negotiations have resulted in compensation adjustments for union employees retroactive to the fourth quarter.

AICPA.aq.sub.events.002_17

307. Which of the following factors should an auditor consider most important upon subsequent discovery of facts that existed at the date of the audit report and would have affected the report?

A. The cost-to-benefit ratio of performing additional procedures to better determine the impact of the newly discovered facts.

B. The potential impact on financial statements and associated audit reports for the previous five years.

C. The client's willingness to pay additional fees for the additional procedures to be performed.

D. The client's willingness to issue revised financial statements or other disclosures to persons known to be relying on the financial statement.

AICPA.101103AUD

308. An auditor should be aware of subsequent events that provide evidence concerning conditions that did not exist at year end but arose after year end. These events may be important to the auditor because they may

A. Require adjustments to the financial statements as of the year end.

B. Have been recorded based on preliminary accounting estimates.

C. Require disclosure to keep the financial statements from being misleading.

D. Have been recorded based on year-end tests for asset obsolescence.

AICPA.130701AUD

309. An auditor is considering whether the omission of the confirmation of investments impairs the auditor's ability to support a previously expressed unmodified opinion. The auditor need not perform this omitted procedure if

A. The results of alternative procedures that were performed compensate for the omission.

B. The auditor's assessed level of detection risk is low.

C. The omission is documented in a communication with the audit committee.

D. No individual investment is material to the financial statements taken as a whole.

AICPA.130704AUD

310. Subsequent to issuing a report on audited financial statements, a CPA discovers that the accounts receivable confirmation process omitted a number of accounts that are material, in the aggregate. Which of the following actions should the CPA take immediately?

A. Bring the matter to the attention of the board of directors or audit committee.
B. Withdraw the auditor's report from those persons currently relying on it.
C. Perform alternative procedures to verify account balances.
D. Discuss the potential financial statement adjustments with client management.

Going Concern Issues

AICPA.111193AUD-SIM

311. An auditor concludes that there is substantial doubt about an entity's ability to continue as a going concern for a reasonable period of time. The entity's financial statements adequately disclose its financial difficulties. Under these circumstances, the auditor's report is required to include an emphasis-of-matter paragraph that specifically uses the phrase(s)

	"Except for the Effects of Such Adjustments"	"Possible Discontinuance of the Entity's Operations"
A.	Yes	Yes
B.	Yes	No
C.	No	Yes
D.	No	No

AICPA.120702AUD

312. Which of the following audit procedures *most likely* would assist an auditor in identifying conditions and events that may indicate there could be substantial doubt about an entity's ability to continue as a going concern?

A. Confirmation of accounts receivable from principal customers.
B. Reconciliation of interest expense with debt outstanding.
C. Confirmation of bank balances.
D. Review of compliance with terms of debt agreements.

AICPA.120709AUD

313. An auditor should consider which of the following when evaluating the ability of a company to continue as a going concern?

A. Audit fees.
B. Future assurance services.

C. Management's plans for disposal of assets.
D. A lawsuit for which judgment is NOT anticipated for 18 months.

AICPA.130703AUD

314. An auditor has substantial doubt about the entity's ability to continue as a going concern for a reasonable period of time because of negative cash flows and working capital deficiencies. Under these circumstances, the auditor would be most concerned about the

A. Control environment factors that affect the organizational structure.
B. Correlation of detection risk and inherent risk.
C. Effectiveness of the entity's internal control activities.
D. Possible effects on the entity's financial statements.

AICPA.951159AUD-AU

315. Cooper, CPA, believes there is substantial doubt about the ability of Zero Corp. to continue as a going concern for a reasonable period of time. In evaluating Zero's plans for dealing with the adverse effects of future conditions and events, Cooper *most likely* would consider, as a mitigating factor, Zero's plans to

A. Discuss with lenders the terms of all debt and loan agreements.
B. Strengthen internal controls over cash disbursements.
C. Purchase production facilities currently being leased from a related party.
D. Postpone expenditures for research and development projects.

Audit Evidence: Specific Audit Areas

Introduction to Auditing Individual Areas

AICPA.101145AUD

316. Confirmation procedures applicable to assets (e.g., accounts receivable) fundamentally address which assertion associated with account balances at the end of the period?

A. Existence.
B. Completeness.
C. Presentation and disclosure.
D. Valuation and allocation.

AICPA.101146AUD

317. Which of the following is **not** an assertion associated with account balances at the end of the period?

    A. Valuation and allocation.
    B. Rights and obligations.
    C. Classification.
    D. Existence.

AICPA.101147AUD

318. There are certain substantive auditing procedures that might appropriately be performed when auditing any element of the financial statements, particularly balance-sheet elements. Which of the following is **not** a substantive procedure potentially applicable to every balance-sheet element?

    A. Reviewing the accounting records for anything that appears to be unusual.
    B. Performing tests of control to evaluate the effectiveness of relevant controls.
    C. Making appropriate inquiries of management or other client personnel about matters related to the particular balance-sheet element.
    D. Agreeing the financial statement elements to the underlying accounting records, such as the entity's general ledger.

Cash

AICPA.020408AUD-AU

319. On receiving a client's bank cut-off statement, an auditor *most likely* would trace

    A. Prior-year checks listed in the cut-off statement to the year-end outstanding checklist.
    B. Deposits in transit listed in the cut-off statement to the year-end bank reconciliation.
    C. Checks dated after year end listed in the cut-off statement to the year-end outstanding checklist.
    D. Deposits recorded in the cash receipts journal after year end to the cut-off statement.

AICPA.020417AUD-AU

320. Which of the following characteristics *most likely* would be indicative of check kiting?

    A. High turnover of employees who have access to cash.
    B. Many large checks that are recorded on Mondays.

    C. Low average balance compared to high level of deposits.
    D. Frequent ATM checking account withdrawals.

AICPA.070611AUD

321. Which of the following procedures would an auditor *most likely* perform in auditing the statement of cash flows?

    A. Reconcile the amounts included in the statement of cash flows to the other financial statements' amounts.
    B. Vouch a sample of cash receipts and disbursements for the last few days of the current year.
    C. Reconcile the cut-off bank statement to the proof of cash to verify the accuracy of the year-end cash balance.
    D. Confirm the amounts included in the statement of cash flows with the entity's financial institution.

AICPA.101125AUD

322. Which of the following would be a consideration in planning a sample for a test of subsequent cash receipts?

    A. Preliminary judgments about materiality levels.
    B. The amount of bad debt write-offs in the prior year.
    C. The size of the intercompany receivable balance.
    D. The auditor's allowable risk of assessing control risk is too low.

AICPA.111175AUD

323. An auditor has identified the controller's review of the bank reconciliation as a control to test. In connection with this test, the auditor interviews the controller to understand the specific data reviewed on the reconciliation. In addition, the auditor verifies that the bank reconciliation is properly prepared by the accountant and reviewed by the controller, as evidenced by their respective sign-offs. Which of the following types of audit procedures do these actions illustrate?

    A. Observation and inspection of records.
    B. Confirmation and re-performance.
    C. Inquiry and inspection of records.
    D. Analytical procedures and re-performance.

Performing Further Procedures and Obtaining Evidence

Accounts Receivable

AICPA.aq.acct.rec.001_17

324. Which of the following procedures is performed first for unreturned positive confirmations of accounts receivable?

   A. Comparing current sales with budgeted sales.
   B. Sending second requests for confirmation of accounts receivable.
   C. Performing subsequent procedures.
   D. Asking the client to obtain additional correspondence from the customers.

AICPA.070610AUD

325. Which of the following strategies would be *most likely* to improve the response rate of the confirmations of accounts receivable?

   A. Restrict the selection of accounts to be confirmed to those customers with large balances.
   B. Include a list of items or invoices that constitute the customers' account balances.
   C. Explain to customers that discrepancies will be investigated by an independent third party.
   D. Ask customers to respond to the confirmation requests directly to the auditor by fax.

AICPA.120713AUD

326. An auditor is required to confirm accounts receivable if the accounts receivable balances are

   A. Older than the prior year.
   B. Material to the financial statements.
   C. Smaller than expected.
   D. Subject to valuation estimates.

AICPA.130732AUD

327. While performing interim audit procedures of accounts receivable, numerous unexpected errors are found resulting in a change of risk assessment. Which of the following audit responses would be most appropriate?

   A. Move detailed analytical procedures from year end to interim.
   B. Increase the dollar threshold of vouching customer invoices.
   C. Send negative accounts receivable confirmations instead of positive accounts receivable confirmations.
   D. Use more experienced audit team members to perform year-end testing.

AICPA.aq.acct.rec.002_18

328. During a recent audit of the revenue cycle, a CPA found the client had $1 million in accounts receivable recorded for fictitious customers. Which of the following tests *most likely* facilitated identification of the fraud?

   A. Reviewing the segregation of duties for staff who had responsibility for sales, shipping, and invoicing.
   B. Reviewing the support for open sales orders not yet shipped at December 31.
   C. Sending positive confirmations to all of the client's customers with balances on December 31.
   D. Examining the reconciliation between the subsidiary ledger and the general ledger control account.

assess.AICPA.AUD.acct.rec-0005

329. Which of the following procedures would an auditor *most likely* perform to identify unusual sales transactions?

   A. Tracing credits in the accounts receivable ledger to source documentation.
   B. Performing a trend analysis of quarterly sales.
   C. Examining duplicate sales invoices for credit approval by the credit manager.
   D. Tracing cash receipt entries to the bank statement deposit for amount and date.

Inventory

AICPA.aq.inventory.001_17

330. Which of the following control objectives is achieved by reviewing and testing control procedures over physical inventory count?

   A. Validation of purchase transactions.
   B. Verification of existence of inventory.
   C. Authorization of the manufacturing orders.
   D. Posting and summarization of inventory transactions.

AICPA.070619AUD

331. To obtain assurance that all inventory items in a client's inventory listing are valid, an auditor *most likely* would agree

   A. Inventory tags noted during the auditor's observation to items listed in receiving reports and vendors' invoices.
   B. Items listed in receiving reports and vendor's invoices to the inventory listing.
   C. Inventory tags noted during the auditor's observation to items in the inventory listing.
   D. Items in the inventory listing to inventory tags and the auditor's recorded count sheets.

AICPA Release Questions are Copyright 2019 American Institute of CPAs. All rights reserved. Used with permission.

51

AICPA.101094AUD

332. Which of the following procedures would be most appropriate for testing the completeness assertion as it applies to inventory?

   A. Scanning perpetual inventory, production, and purchasing records.
   B. Examining paid vendor's invoices.
   C. Tracing inventory items from the tag listing back to the physical inventory quantities.
   D. Performing cut-off procedures for shipping and receiving.

AICPA.111171AUD

333. The purpose of tracing a sample of inventory tags to a client's computerized listing of inventory items is to determine whether the inventory items

   A. Represented by tags were included on the listing.
   B. Included on the listing were properly counted.
   C. Represented by tags were reduced to lower of cost or market.
   D. Included in the listing were properly valued.

assess.AICPA.AUD.inventory-0040

334. A senior auditor conducted a dual-purpose test on a client's invoice to determine whether the invoice was approved and to ascertain the amount and other terms of the invoice. Which of the following lists two tests that the auditor performed?

   A. Substantive procedures and analytical procedures.
   B. Substantive analytical procedures and tests of controls.
   C. Tests of controls and tests of details.
   D. Tests of details and substantive procedures.

Investments in Securities and Derivative Instruments

AICPA.070612AUD

335. In establishing the existence and ownership of long-term investments in the form of publicly traded stock, an auditor *most likely* would inspect the securities or

   A. Correspond with the investee company to verify the number of shares owned.
   B. Confirm the number of shares owned that are held by an independent custodian.
   C. Apply analytical procedures to the dividend income and investments accounts.
   D. Inspect the cash receipts journal for amounts that could represent the sale of securities.

AICPA.090792.AUD-AU

336. An auditor is testing the reasonableness of dividend income from investments in publicly held companies. The auditor *most likely* would compute the amount that should have been received and recorded by the client by

   A. Reading the details of the board of directors' meetings.
   B. Confirming the details with the investee companies' registrars.
   C. Electronically accessing the details of dividend records on the Internet.
   D. Examining the details of the client's most recent cut-off bank statement.

AICPA.aq.invest.secur.001_18

337. How should an auditor verify the valuation of marketable securities at the balance sheet date?

   A. Confirm all securities with the related custodians and test interest income.
   B. Observe the inventory count of all securities at the balance sheet date.
   C. Compare the prices of the securities to published closing prices at the balance sheet date.
   D. Inquire of management that securities are valued at fair value.

AICPA.950544AUD-AU

338. In confirming with an outside agent, such as a financial institution, that the agent is holding investment securities in the client's name, an auditor would *most likely* gather evidence in support of management's financial statement assertions of existence or occurrence and

   A. Valuation or allocation.
   B. Rights and obligations.
   C. Completeness.
   D. Presentation and disclosure.

Fixed Assets

AICPA.070603AUD

339. An analysis of which of the following accounts would best aid in verifying that all fixed assets have been capitalized?

   A. Cash.
   B. Depreciation expense.
   C. Property tax expense.
   D. Repairs and maintenance.

AICPA.070640AUD

340. An auditor's principal objective in analyzing repairs and maintenance expense accounts is to

A. Determine that all obsolete plant and equipment assets were written off before the year end.
B. Verify that all recorded plant and equipment assets actually exist.
C. Discover expenditures that were expensed, but should have been capitalized.
D. Identify plant and equipment assets that cannot be repaired and should be written off.

AICPA.130702AUD

341. Which of the following explanations *most likely* would satisfy an auditor who questions management about significant debits to accumulated depreciation accounts in the current year?

A. Prior years' depreciation expenses were erroneously understated.
B. Current year's depreciation expense was erroneously understated.
C. The estimated remaining useful lives of plant assets were revised upward.
D. Plant assets were retired during the current year.

AICPA.130714AUD

342. Which of the following procedures would an auditor *most likely* complete to test the existence assertion of property, plant and equipment?

A. Obtaining a listing of all current-year additions, vouching significant additions to original invoices, and determining that they have been placed in service.
B. Obtaining a detailed fixed-asset register and ensuring items are appropriately capitalized.
C. Obtaining a listing of current-year additions and verifying that items are recorded in the proper period.
D. Obtaining a detailed fixed-asset register and ensuring depreciation methods are applied consistently.

AICPA.951149AUD-AU

343. Which of the following explanations *most likely* would satisfy an auditor who questions management about significant debits to the accumulated depreciation accounts?

A. The estimated remaining useful lives of plant assets were revised upward.
B. Plant assets were retired during the year.

C. The prior year's depreciation expense was erroneously understated.
D. Overhead allocations were revised at year end.

Current Liabilities

AICPA.940547AUD-AU

344. Which of the following audit procedures is best for identifying unrecorded trade accounts payable?

A. Reviewing cash disbursements recorded subsequent to the balance sheet date to determine whether the related payables apply to the prior period.
B. Investigating payables recorded just prior to and just subsequent to the balance sheet date to determine whether they are supported by receiving reports.
C. Examining unusual relationships between monthly accounts payable balances and recorded cash payments.
D. Reconciling vendors' statements to the file of receiving reports to identify items received just prior to the balance sheet date.

AICPA.941153AUD-AU

345. When using confirmations to provide evidence about the completeness assertion for accounts payable, the appropriate population *most likely* would be

A. Vendors with whom the entity has previously done business.
B. Amounts recorded in the accounts payable subsidiary ledger.
C. Payees of checks drawn in the month after the year end.
D. Invoices filed in the entity's open invoice file.

AICPA.950573AUD-AU

346. Which of the following procedures would an auditor *least likely* perform before the balance sheet date?

A. Confirmation of accounts payable.
B. Observation of merchandise inventory.
C. Assessment of control risk.
D. Identification of related parties.

AICPA.951147AUD-AU

347. Which of the following procedures would an auditor *most likely* perform in searching for unrecorded liabilities?

    A. Trace a sample of accounts payable entries recorded just before year end to the unmatched receiving report file.
    B. Compare a sample of purchase orders issued just after year end with the year-end accounts payable trial balance.
    C. Vouch a sample of cash disbursements recorded just after year end to receiving reports and vendor invoices.
    D. Scan the cash disbursements entries recorded just before year end for indications of unusual transactions.

AICPA.951148AUD-AU

348. An auditor traced a sample of purchase orders and the related receiving reports to the purchases journal and the cash disbursements journal. The purpose of this substantive audit procedure *most likely* was to

    A. Identify unusually large purchases that should be investigated further.
    B. Verify that cash disbursements were for goods actually received.
    C. Determine that purchases were properly recorded.
    D. Test whether payments were for goods actually ordered.

Long-term Liabilities

AICPA.090315AUD-SIM

349. The permanent file section of the audit documentation that is kept for a continuing audit engagement *most likely* would contain

    A. The most recent lawyer's letter applicable to unresolved litigation.
    B. The most recent time budget for the audit engagement.
    C. Copies (or abstracts) of the entity's lease agreements.
    D. Copies of the entity's most recent tax returns.

AICPA.090316AUD-SIM

350. In the following schedule of analysis related to long-term liabilities, the tickmark € *most likely* is associated with which particular auditing procedure?

Wrigleyville Company

Schedule of Long-Term Debt

As of 12/31/X1

Payee	Due Date	Face Amount	Beginning Balance	Additions	Payments	Ending Balance
Second City Bank - Line of Credit	11/4/X7	$10,000,000	$500,000 ø	$800,000 ∆	$400,000 €	$900,000
4% bonds payable	10/28/X5	$3,000,000	$750,000 ø		$250,000 €	$500,000
5% bonds payable	2/12/X8	$9,000,000	$3,250,000 ø		$250,000 €	$3,000,000
Total			$4,500,000	$800,000	$900,000	$4,400,000
Less: current portion of long-term debt						500,000 ©
						$3,900,000 G

    A. Agreed to the cash disbursements journal and traced to the applicable bank statement.
    B. Agreed to the general ledger.
    C. Recomputed interest expense.
    D. Agreed the current portion of long-term debt to the loan agreement's payment schedule.

AICPA.090317AUD-SIM

351. In the following schedule of analysis related to accrued interest payable associated with long-term liabilities, the tickmark ¥ *most likely* is associated with which particular auditing procedure?

Wrigleyville Company

Schedule of Accrued Interest Payable

As of 12/31/X1

Payee	Due Date	Beginning Balance	20X1 Expense	Payments	Ending Balance
Second City Bank - Line of Credit	11/4/X7	$2,500 Ψ	$10,250 ¥	$11,500 €	$1,250
4% bonds payable	10/28/X5	$7,500 Ψ	$22,500 ¥	$25,000 €	$5,000
5 % bonds payable	2/12/X8	$22,500 Ψ	$100,750 ¥	$120,000 €	$3,250
Total		$32,500	$133,500	$156,500	$9,500 G

A. Agreed to the cash disbursements journal and traced to the applicable bank statement.
B. Agreed to the general ledger.
C. Recomputed interest expense.
D. Agreed to the prior year's audit documentation.

AICPA.941160AUD-AU

352. In auditing long-term bonds payable, an auditor *most likely* would

A. Perform analytical procedures on the bond premium and discount accounts.
B. Examine documentation of assets purchased with bond proceeds for liens.
C. Compare interest expense with the bond payable amount for reasonableness.
D. Confirm the existence of individual bondholders at year end.

Stockholders' Equity

AICPA.060657AUD

353. When a company's stock record books are maintained by an outside registrar or transfer agent, the auditor should obtain confirmation from the registrar or transfer agent concerning the

A. Amount of dividends paid to related parties.
B. Expected proceeds from stock subscriptions receivable.
C. Number of shares issued and outstanding.
D. Proper authorization of stock rights and warrants.

AICPA.980522AUD-AU

354. In auditing a client's retained earnings account, an auditor should determine whether there are any restrictions on retained earnings that result from loans, agreements, or state law.

This procedure is designed to corroborate management's financial statement assertion of

A. Valuation or allocation.
B. Existence or occurrence.
C. Completeness.
D. Rights and obligations.

AICPA.990421AUD-AU

355. An auditor usually obtains evidence of stockholders' equity transactions by reviewing the entity's

A. Minutes of board of directors' meetings.
B. Transfer agent's records.
C. Cancelled stock certificates.
D. Treasury stock certificate book.

Payroll

AICPA.020414AUD-AU

356. An auditor reviews the reconciliation of payroll tax forms that a client is responsible for filing in order to

A. Verify that payroll taxes are deducted from employees' gross pay.
B. Determine whether internal control activities are operating effectively.
C. Uncover fictitious employees who are receiving payroll checks.
D. Identify potential liabilities for unpaid payroll taxes.

AICPA.950554AUD-AU

357. When control risk is assessed as low for assertions related to payroll, substantive tests of payroll balances *most likely* would be limited to applying analytical procedures and

A. Observing the distribution of paychecks.
B. Footing and crossfooting the payroll register.
C. Inspecting payroll tax returns.
D. Recalculating payroll accruals.

AICPA.951150AUD-AU

358. Which of the following circumstances *most likely* would cause an auditor to suspect an employee payroll fraud scheme?

A. There are significant unexplained variances between standard and actual labor costs.
B. Payroll checks are disbursed by the same employee each payday.
C. Employee time cards are approved by individual departmental supervisors.
D. A separate payroll bank account is maintained on an imprest basis.

AICPA.970417AUD-AU

359. Which of the following comparisons would an auditor *most likely* make in evaluating an entity's costs and expenses?

A. The current year's accounts receivable with the prior year's accounts receivable.
B. The current year's payroll expense with the prior year's payroll expense.
C. The budgeted current year's sales with the prior year's sales.
D. The budgeted current year's warranty expense with the current year's contingent liabilities.

Audit Sampling

Introduction to Sampling

AICPA.101131AUD

360. When performing a substantive test of a random sample of cash disbursements, an auditor is supplied with a photocopy of vendor invoices supporting the disbursements for one particular vendor, rather than the original invoices. The auditor is told that the vendor's original invoices have been misplaced. What should the auditor do in response to this situation?

A. Randomly increase the number of items in the substantive test to increase the reliance that may be placed on the overall test.
B. Reevaluate the risk of fraud and design alternate tests for the related transactions.
C. Increase testing by agreeing more of the payments to this particular vendor to the photocopies of its invoices.
D. Count the missing original documents as misstatements and project the total amount of the error based on the size of the population and the dollar amount of the errors.

AICPA.130736AUD

361. Which of the following statements about audit sampling risks is correct for a nonissuer?

A. Nonsampling risk arises from the possibility that, when a substantive test is restricted to a sample, conclusions might be different than if the auditor had tested each item in the population.
B. Nonsampling risk can arise because an auditor failed to recognize misstatements.
C. Sampling risk is derived from the uncertainty in applying audit procedures to specific risks.
D. Sampling risk includes the possibility of selecting audit procedures that are not appropriate to achieve the specific objective.

AICPA.941156AUD-AU

362. Which of the following sample planning factors would influence the sample size for a substantive test of details for a specific account?

	Expected Amount of Misstatements	Measure of Tolerable Misstatement
A.	No	No
B.	Yes	Yes
C.	No	Yes
D.	Yes	No

AICPA.950536AUD-AU

363. An advantage that using statistical sampling methods have over nonstatistical sampling methods in tests of controls is that the statistical methods

A. Can more easily convert the sample into a dual-purpose test useful for substantive testing.
B. Eliminate the need to use judgment in determining appropriate sample sizes.
C. Afford greater assurance than a nonstatistical sample of equal size.
D. Provide an objective basis for quantitatively evaluating sample risk.

Attributes Sampling

AICPA.aq.att.sample.002_18

364. Which of the following types of sampling allows an auditor to quantify sampling risk?

A. Stratified nonstatistical.
B. Haphazard
C. Attribute
D. Block

AICPA.aq.att.sample.001_17

365. Which of the following audit procedures *most likely* will involve sampling?

A. Risk assessment procedures performed to obtain an understanding of internal control.

B. Tests of automated application controls when effective information technology general controls are present.

C. Analyses of controls to determine the appropriate segregation of duties.

D. Testing of process for approval of credit to customers for sales on account.

AICPA.090797.AUD-AU

366. In attribute sampling, a 25% change in which of the following factors will have the smallest effect on the size of the sample?

A. Tolerable rate of deviation.

B. Number of items in the population.

C. Degree of assurance desired.

D. Planned assessed level of control risk.

AICPA.120726AUD

367. For which of the following audit tests would an auditor *most likely* use attribute sampling?

A. Inspecting purchase orders for proper approval by supervisors.

B. Making an independent estimate of recorded payroll expense.

C. Determining that all payables are recorded at year end.

D. Selecting accounts receivable for confirmation of account balances.

AICPA.120740AUD

368. Which of the following statements is generally correct about the sample size in statistical sampling when testing internal controls?

A. As the population size doubles, the sample size should increase by about 67.

B. The sample size is inversely proportional to the expected error rate.

C. There is NO relationship between the tolerable error rate and the sample size.

D. The population size has little or NO effect on the sample size.

AICPA.940544AUD-AU

369. The sample size of a test of controls varies inversely with

	Expected Population Deviation Rate	Tolerable Rate
A.	Yes	Yes
B.	No	No
C.	Yes	No
D.	No	Yes

Variables Sampling

AICPA.111199AUD

370. An auditor discovers that an account balance believed not to be materially misstated based on an audit sample was materially misstated based on the total population of the account balance. This is an example of which of the following types of sampling risks?

A. Incorrect rejection.

B. Incorrect acceptance.

C. Assessing control risk too low.

D. Assessing control risk too high.

AICPA.941154AUD-AU

371. Which of the following sampling methods would be used to estimate a numerical measurement of a population, such as a dollar value?

A. Attributes sampling.

B. Stop-or-go sampling.

C. Variables sampling.

D. Random number sampling.

AICPA.950551AUD-AU

372. The use of the ratio estimation sampling technique is most effective when

A. The calculated audit amounts are approximately proportional to the client's book amounts.

B. A relatively small number of differences exist in the population.

C. Estimating populations whose records consist of quantities, but not book values.

D. Large overstatement differences and large understatement differences exist in the population.

AICPA.951143AUD-AU

373. How would increases in tolerable misstatement and assessed level of control risk affect the sample size in a substantive test of details?

	Increase in Tolerable Misstatement	Increase in Assessed Level of Control Risk
A.	Increase sample size	Increase sample size
B.	Increase sample size	Decrease sample size
C.	Decrease sample size	Increase sample size
D.	Decrease sample size	Decrease sample size

assess.AICPA.AUD.var.sample-0012

374. In an audit of a nonissuer's financial statements, projected misstatement is

A. The likely amount of misstatement in the subsequent period's financial statements if a control is **not** properly implemented.

B. An auditor's best estimate of misstatements in a population extrapolated from misstatements identified in an audit sample.

C. The only amount that the auditor considers in evaluating materiality and fairness of the financial statements.

D. An auditor's best estimate, before performing audit procedures, of misstatements that the auditor expects to find during the audit.

Probability-Proportional-to-Size (PPS) Sampling

AICPA.090790.AUD-AU

375. Which of the following is the primary objective of probability proportional to sample size?

A. To identify overstatement errors.

B. To increase the proportion of smaller-value items in the sample.

C. To identify items where controls were not properly applied.

D. To identify zero and negative balances.

AICPA.140404AUD-SIM

376. In a PPS sampling application, the sampling interval was $6,000. The auditor discovered that a selected account receivable having a recorded amount of $5,000 had an audit amount of $1,000. What was the projected error associated with this sample?

A. $4,000

B. $1,200

C. $4,800

D. $3,200

AICPA.140405AUD-SIM

377. Hill has decided to use (PPS) sampling, sometimes called dollar-unit sampling, in the audit of a client's accounts receivable balances. Hill plans to use the following PPS sampling table:

Reliability Factors for Errors of Overstatement

Number of Overstatements	Risk of Incorrect Acceptance				
	1%	5%	10%	15%	20%
0	4.61	3.00	2.31	1.90	1.61
1	6.64	4.75	3.89	3.38	3.00
2	8.41	6.30	5.33	4.72	4.28
3	10.05	7.76	6.69	6.02	5.52
4	11.61	9.16	8.00	7.27	6.73

ADDITIONAL INFORMATION

Tolerable misstatement (net of the effect of expected misstatements)	$24,000
Risk of incorrect acceptance	20%
Number of misstatements allowed	1
Recorded amount of accounts receivable	$240,000
Number of accounts	360

What sample size should Hill use?

A. 120

B. 108

C. 60

D. 30

AICPA.920530AUD-AU

378. In a probability-proportional-to-size sample with a sampling interval of $5,000, an auditor discovered that a selected account receivable with a recorded amount of $10,000 had an audit amount of $8,000.

If this were the only error discovered by the auditor, the projected error of this sample would be

A. $1,000

B. $2,000

C. $4,000

D. $5,000

IT (Computer) Auditing

IT Controls—General Controls

AICPA.010418AUD-AU

379. In building an electronic data interchange (EDI) system, what process is used to determine which elements in the entity's computer system correspond to the standard data elements?

   A. Mapping.
   B. Translation.
   C. Encryption.
   D. Decoding.

AICPA.010506AUD-AU

380. Which of the following procedures would an entity *most likely* include in its disaster recovery plan?

   A. Convert all data from EDI format to an internal company format.
   B. Maintain a Trojan horse program to prevent illicit activity.
   C. Develop an auxiliary power supply to provide uninterrupted electricity.
   D. Store duplicate copies of files in a location away from the computer center.

AICPA.010519AUD-AU

381. Which of the following is a password security problem?

   A. Users are assigned passwords when accounts are created, but do not change them.
   B. Users have accounts on several systems with different passwords.
   C. Users copy their passwords onto notepaper, which is kept in their wallets.
   D. Users select passwords that are not listed in any online dictionary.

AICPA.070605AUD

382. The ultimate purpose of assessing control risk is to contribute to the auditor's evaluation of the risk that

   A. Specific internal control activities are not operating as designed.
   B. The collective effect of the control environment may not achieve the control objectives.
   C. Tests of controls may fail to identify activities relevant to assertions.
   D. Material misstatements may exist in the financial statements.

assess.AICPA.AUD.it.con.gen-0007

383. Which of the following tasks can be achieved using generalized audit software?

   A. Determining acceptable risk levels for substantive testing of account balances.
   B. Filtering data based on accounts receivable data recording.
   C. Detecting transactions that may be suspicious due to alteration of data input.
   D. Assessing likelihood of fraud based on input of fraud risk factors.

IT Controls—Application Controls

AICPA.941137AUD-AU

384. Misstatements in a batch computer system caused by incorrect programs or data may not be detected immediately because

   A. Errors in some transactions may cause rejection of other transactions in the batch.
   B. The identification of errors in input data is typically not part of the program.
   C. There are time delays in processing transactions in a batch system.
   D. The processing of transactions in a batch system is not uniform.

AICPA.941138AUD-AU

385. Which of the following controls is a processing control designed to ensure the reliability and accuracy of data processing?

	Limit Test	Validity Check Test
A.	Yes	Yes
B.	No	No
C.	No	Yes
D.	Yes	No

AICPA.951103AUD-AU

386. Able Co. uses an online sales order processing system to process its sales transactions. Able's sales data are electronically sorted and subjected to edit checks.

A direct output of the edit checks *most likely* would be a

   A. Report of all missing sales invoices.
   B. File of all rejected sales transactions.
   C. Printout of all user code numbers and passwords.
   D. List of all voided shipping documents.

AICPA.951110AUD-AU

387. Which of the following is an example of a validity check?

A. The computer ensures that a numerical amount in a record does not exceed some predetermined amount.
B. As the computer corrects errors and data are successfully resubmitted to the system, the causes of the errors are printed out.
C. The computer flags any transmission for which the control field value did not match that of an existing file record.
D. After data for a transaction are entered, the computer sends certain data back to the terminal for comparison with data originally sent.

IT Evidence—Gathering Procedures

AICPA.aq.it.evid.pro.001_17

388. As part of a fraud audit, a CPA wishes to identify employees with invalid Social Security numbers in the client's payroll-transaction data. Which of the following audit tests of controls using computer-assisted audit techniques would best meet the objective?

A. Obtaining statistics on the population of the payroll file to identify unusual pay amounts to employees.
B. Comparing Social Security numbers paid in the payroll transaction file to a file of government- authorized Social Security numbers.
C. Randomly selecting 25 payments from the payroll report and comparing the results to employee Social Security cards in the human resources records.
D. Comparing the payroll transaction file to the employee master file to extract payments to employees who are **not** in the employee master file.

AICPA.aq.it.evid.pro.002_17

389. An auditor will *most likely* use computer-assisted audit techniques, rather than manual techniques, when it is necessary to

A. Examine all data in an accounts payable file.
B. Review approval of dividends.
C. Verify unrecorded legal liabilities.
D. Assess compliance with policies and procedures related to information security.

AICPA.010415AUD-AU

390. An auditor who wishes to capture an entity's data as transactions are processed and continuously test the entity's computerized information system *most likely* would use which of the following techniques?

A. Snapshot application.
B. Embedded audit module.
C. Integrated data check.
D. Test data generator.

AICPA.010517AUD-AU

391. Which of the following computer-assisted auditing techniques processes client input data on a controlled program under the auditor's control to test controls in the computer system?

A. Test data.
B. Review of program logic.
C. Integrated test facility.
D. Parallel simulation.

AICPA.020420AUD-AU

392. Which of the following is the primary reason that many auditors hesitate to use embedded audit modules?

A. Embedded audit modules cannot be protected from computer viruses.
B. Auditors are required to monitor embedded audit modules continuously to obtain valid results.
C. Embedded audit modules can easily be modified through management tampering.
D. Auditors are required to be involved in the system design of the application to be monitored.

AICPA.070628AUD

393. After testing a client's internal control activities, an auditor discovers a number of significant deficiencies in the operation of a client's internal controls. Under these circumstances the auditor *most likely* would

A. Issue a disclaimer of opinion about the internal controls as part of the auditor's report.
B. Increase the assessment of control risk and increase the extent of substantive tests.
C. Issue a qualified opinion of this finding as part of the auditor's report.
D. Withdraw from the audit because the internal controls are ineffective.

AICPA.090794.AUD-AU

394. In auditing an entity's computerized payroll transactions, an auditor would be *least likely* to use test data to test controls concerning

A. Overpayment of employees for hours not worked.
B. Control and distribution of unclaimed checks.
C. Withholding of taxes and Social Security contributions.
D. Missing employee identification numbers.

Other IT Considerations

AICPA.010407AUD-AU

395. Which of the following characteristics distinguishes electronic data interchange (EDI) from other forms of electronic commerce?

A. EDI transactions are formatted using standards that are uniform worldwide.
B. EDI transactions need not comply with generally accepted accounting principles.
C. EDI transactions are ordinarily processed without the Internet.
D. EDI transactions are usually recorded without security or privacy concerns.

AICPA.010417AUD-AU

396. Which of the following computer-assisted auditing techniques processes client input data on a controlled program under the auditor's control to test controls in the computer system?

A. Test data.
B. Review of program logic.
C. Integrated test facility.
D. Parallel simulation.

AICPA.010505AUD-AU

397. Which of the following is a computer program that appears to be legitimate, but performs some illicit activity when it is run?

A. Hoax virus.
B. Web crawler.
C. Trojan horse.
D. Killer application.

AICPA.010518AUD-AU

398. In building an electronic data interchange (EDI) system, what process is used to determine which elements in the entity's computer system correspond to the standard data elements?

A. Mapping.
B. Translation.
C. Encryption.
D. Decoding.

AICPA.990514AUD-AU

399. Which of the following are essential elements of the audit trail in an electronic data interchange (EDI) system?

A. Network and sender/recipient acknowledgments.
B. Message directories and header segments.
C. Contingency and disaster recovery plans.
D. Trading partner security and mailbox codes.

Forming Conclusions and Reporting

Audit Reports

Introduction to Audit Reports

AICPA.aq.intro.aud.rep.001_18

400. A former client requests a predecessor auditor to reissue the prior-year's audit report in connection with the issuance of comparative financial statements by the client. What is the predecessor auditor's responsibility?

A. Review the previous report and make the necessary changes.
B. Consult with the client's legal counsel to determine available remedies.
C. Read the current report, compare it to the previous report, and obtain a letter of representation from the successor auditor.
D. Audit the current statements.

AICPA.951168AUD-AU

401. GAAS require the auditor's report to contain either an expression of opinion regarding the financial statements or an assertion to the effect that an opinion cannot be expressed.

The objective of this requirement is to prevent

A. An auditor from expressing different opinions on each of the basic financial statements.
B. Restrictions on the scope of the audit, whether imposed by the client or by the inability to obtain evidence.
C. Misinterpretations regarding the degree of responsibility the auditor is assuming.
D. An auditor from reporting on one basic financial statement and not the others.

AICPA.980421AUD-AU

402. When issuing an unmodified opinion, the auditor who evaluates the audit findings should be satisfied that the

A. Amount of known misstatement is documented in the management representation letter.
B. Estimate of the total likely misstatement is less than a material amount.
C. Amount of known misstatement is acknowledged and recorded by the client.
D. Estimate of the total likely misstatement includes the adjusting entries already recorded by the client.

PCAOB on Audit Reports

aq.pcaob.aud.rep.0001_0318

403. Form AP, which must be filed with the PCAOB for every audit of an issuer, addresses each of the following matters **except** for

A. The year when the auditor first began serving consecutively as the company's auditor.
B. The extent of participation of any other accounting firm whose participation in the audit accounts for 5% or more of the total audit hours involved with the engagement.
C. The name of the engagement partner.
D. The number and extent in total of all other accounting firms whose participation in the audit accounts for less than 5% of the total audit hours involved with the engagement.

aq.pcaob.aud.rep.0002_0318

404. Which of the following statements is **not** correct about the auditor's report under PCAOB auditing standards?

A. The auditor's opinion is expressed at the beginning of the audit report.
B. The date of the auditor's report has been changed to the date that the issuer filed the applicable financial statements with the Securities and Exchange Commission.
C. Each section of the audit report must have an appropriate label.
D. Critical audit matters must be identified and discussed in the auditor's report.

aq.pcaob.aud.rep.0004_0318

405. For each critical audit matter identified in the current year's audit, PCAOB auditing standards require the auditor's report to include communication of all of the following, except for

A. Considerations that caused the auditor to identify the matter as a critical audit matter.
B. A statement regarding the audit committee's response whether they agree or disagree with the classification of the matter as a critical audit matter.
C. Description of how the critical audit matter was addressed during the audit.
D. Reference to the financial statement accounts or disclosures involved.

Audits of Group Financial Statements

AICPA.990415AUD-AU

406. Which of the following procedures would the group auditor *most likely* perform after deciding to make reference to a component auditor who audited a subsidiary of the reporting entity?

    A. Review the audit documentation and the audit programs of the component auditor.
    B. Visit the other CPA and discuss the results of the component auditor's procedures.
    C. Make inquiries about the professional reputation and independence of the component auditor.
    D. Determine that the component auditor has a sufficient understanding of the subsidiary's internal control.

assess.AICPA.AUD.audit.group-0046

407. When an auditor of a parent nonissuer is also the auditor of a component, then each of the following factors would ordinarily influence the decision to obtain a separate engagement letter from the component **except**

    A. The legal requirements regarding the appointment of the auditor.
    B. Whether a separate audit report is to be issued on the component.
    C. Whether there has been any turnover of the component's board members.
    D. The degree of independence of the component management from the parent entity.

Emphasis-of-Matter Paragraphs and Other-Matter Paragraphs

AICPA.900512AUD-AU

408. An separate paragraph following the opinion paragraph of an auditor's report describes an uncertainty as follows:

    As discussed in Note X to the financial statements, the Company is a defendant in a lawsuit alleging infringement of certain patent rights and claiming damages. Discovery proceedings are in progress. The ultimate outcome of the litigation cannot presently be determined. Accordingly, no provision for any liability that may result upon adjudication has been made in the accompanying financial statements.

What type of audit report should the auditor issue under these circumstances?

    A. Unmodified.
    B. "Subject to" qualified.
    C. "Except for" qualified.
    D. Disclaimer.

AICPA.951164AUD-AU

409. An auditor *most likely* would express an unmodified opinion and would not add an emphasis-of-matter or other-matter paragraph to the report if the auditor

    A. Wishes to emphasize that the entity had significant transactions with related parties.
    B. Concurs with the entity's change in its method of accounting for inventories.
    C. Discovers that supplementary information required by FASB has been omitted.
    D. Believes that there is a remote likelihood of a material loss resulting from an uncertainty.

Qualified for Scope Limitation

AICPA.070639AUD

410. Under which of the following circumstances would an auditor's expression of an unmodified opinion be inappropriate?

    A. The auditor is unable to obtain the audited financial statements of a significant subsidiary.
    B. The financial statements are prepared on the entity's income tax basis.
    C. There are significant deficiencies in the design and operation of the entity's internal control.
    D. Analytical procedures indicate that many year-end account balances are not comparable with the prior year's balances.

AICPA.101132AUD

411. When qualifying an opinion because of an insufficiency of audit evidence, an auditor should modify the situation in the

	Auditor's Responsibility Section	Notes to the Financial Statements
A.	Yes	Yes
B.	Yes	No
C.	No	Yes
D.	No	No

Qualified for Misstatement

AICPA.120723AUD

412. Zag Co. issues financial statements that present financial position and results of operations but Zag omits the related statement of cash flows. Zag would like to engage Brown, CPA, to audit its financial statements without the statement of cash flows although Brown's access to all of the information underlying the basic financial statements will not be limited. Under these circumstances, Brown *most likely* would

    A. Add an emphasis-of-matter paragraph to the standard auditor's report that justifies the reason for the omission.
    B. Refuse to accept the engagement as proposed because of the client-imposed scope limitation.
    C. Explain to Zag that the omission requires a qualification of the auditor's opinion.
    D. Prepare the statement of cash flows as an accommodation to Zag and express an unmodified opinion.

AICPA.931151AUD-AU

413. When an auditor qualifies an opinion because of inadequate disclosure, the auditor should describe the nature of the omission in a separate basis for qualified opinion paragraph and modify the

	Introductory Paragraph	Management Responsibility Paragraph
A.	Yes	Yes
B.	Yes	No
C.	No	Yes
D.	No	No

Adverse Opinion

AICPA.120728AUD

414. A client has capitalizable leases but refuses to capitalize them in the financial statements. Which of the following reporting options does an auditor have if the amounts pervasively distort the financial statements?

    A. Qualified opinion.
    B. Unmodified opinion.
    C. Disclaimer opinion.
    D. Adverse opinion.

AICPA.951165AUD-AU

415. An auditor would express an unmodified opinion with an emphasis-of-matter paragraph added to the auditor's report for

	An Unjustified Accounting Change	A Material Weakness in the Internal Control Structure
A.	Yes	Yes
B.	Yes	No
C.	No	Yes
D.	No	No

Disclaimer of Opinion

AICPA.900518AUD-AU

416. Under which of the following circumstances would a disclaimer of opinion not be appropriate?

    A. The auditor is engaged after fiscal year-end and is unable to observe physical inventories or apply alternative procedures to verify their balances.
    B. The auditor is unable to determine the amounts associated with illegal acts committed by the client's management.
    C. The financial statements fail to contain adequate disclosure concerning related party transactions.
    D. The client refuses to permit its attorney to furnish information requested in a letter of audit inquiry.

AICPA.900557AUD-AU

417. Morris, CPA, suspects that a pervasive scheme of illegal bribes exists throughout the operations of Worldwide Import-Export, Inc., a new audit client. Morris notified the audit committee and Worldwide's legal counsel, but neither could assist Morris in determining whether the amounts involved were material to the financial statements or whether senior management was involved in the scheme.

Under these circumstances, Morris should

    A. Express an unmodified opinion with a separate emphasis-of-matter paragraph.
    B. Disclaim an opinion on the financial statements.
    C. Express an adverse opinion on the financial statements.
    D. Express an unmodified opinion with a separate other-matter paragraph.

AICPA.931146AUD-AU

418. When disclaiming an opinion due to a client-imposed scope limitation, an auditor should indicate in a separate paragraph why the audit did not comply with generally accepted auditing standards. The auditor should also

	Modify the Auditor's Responsibility Section	Omit the Opinion Paragraph
A.	No	Yes
B.	Yes	Yes
C.	No	No
D.	Yes	No

Consistency of Financial Statements

AICPA.130721AUD

419. When there has been a change in accounting principles, but the effect of the change on the comparability of the financial statements is **not** material, the auditor should

A. Not refer to the change in the auditor's report.
B. Refer to the note in the financial statements that discusses the change.
C. Refer to the change in an emphasis-of-matter paragraph.
D. Explicitly state whether the change conforms with GAAP.

AICPA.140701AUD-SIM

420. An entity changed from the straight-line method to the declining balance method of depreciation for all newly acquired assets. This change has no material effect on the current year's financial statements, but is reasonably certain to have a substantial effect in later years. If the change is disclosed in the notes to the financial statements, the auditor should issue a report with a(n)

A. Qualified opinion.
B. Required "other-matter" paragraph.
C. Unmodified opinion.
D. Disclaimer of opinion.

PCAOB on Evaluating Consistency

AICPA.090647.AUD.SOA.6

421. When there is a change in accounting principle, the auditor should evaluate whether all of the following criteria have been met, except for whether

A. The change has been authorized by those charged with governance.
B. The method of accounting for the effect of the change conforms to GAAP.
C. The disclosures related to the change are adequate.
D. Management has justified that the alternative accounting principle selected is preferable to the previously used accounting principle.

AICPA.090650.AUD.SOA.6

422. If management has not justified that the alternative accounting principle is preferable to an accounting principle previously used and the effect of the change in accounting principle is material to a company's financial statements, the auditor should

A. Decide between a qualified opinion and an adverse opinion.
B. Decide between a qualified opinion and a disclaimer of opinion.
C. Issue an unqualified opinion with an explanatory paragraph.
D. Decide between a disclaimer of opinion and an adverse opinion.

AICPA.090651.AUD.SOA.6

423. An auditor should ordinarily add an explanatory paragraph to the auditor's report to identify a material matter related to

A. A change in reporting entity resulting from a specific transaction or event.
B. A change in accounting principle caused by the issuance of a new authoritative accounting standard that rendered the principle previously used no longer generally accepted.
C. A change in classification in previously issued financial statements.
D. All of the above.

Opening Balances—Initial Audits

AICPA.aq.open.bal.001_17

424. While conducting an audit of a new nonissuer client, an auditor discovers that accounting policies applied in relation to the financial statement opening balances are inconsistent with accounting policies applied during the period under audit. In this scenario, what should the auditor do?

   A. Obtain sufficient appropriate evidence about whether changes in the accounting policies have been appropriately accounted for and adequately presented and disclosed in accordance with the applicable financial reporting framework.
   B. Refrain from placing any reliance on information obtained from the review of the predecessor auditor's audit documentation of the prior period.
   C. Request that management inform the predecessor auditor that the prior-period audited financial statements require revision.
   D. Express a qualified or adverse opinion.

AICPA.130729AUD

425. Which of the following would a successor auditor ask the predecessor auditor to provide after accepting an audit engagement?

   A. Disagreements between the predecessor auditor and management as to significant accounting policies and principles.
   B. The predecessor auditor's understanding of the reasons for the change of auditors.
   C. Facts known to the predecessor auditor that might bear on the integrity of management.
   D. Matters that may facilitate the evaluation of financial reporting consistency between the current and prior years.

Other Information Along with Financial Statements

AICPA.921157AUD-AU

426. When audited financial statements are presented in a client's document containing other information, the auditor should

   A. Perform inquiry and analytical procedures to ascertain whether the other information is reasonable.
   B. Add an emphasis-of-matter paragraph to the auditor's report without changing the opinion on the financial statements.
   C. Perform the appropriate substantive auditing procedures to corroborate the other information.

   D. Read the other information to determine that it is consistent with the audited financial statements.

Supplementary Information Related to Financial Statements

AICPA.950587AUD-AU

427. If supplementary information in a document accompanying the basic financial statements has been subjected to auditing procedures, the auditor may include in the auditor's report on the financial statements an opinion that the accompanying information is fairly stated in

   A. Accordance with generally accepted auditing standards.
   B. Conformity with generally accepted accounting principles.
   C. All material respects in relation to the financial statements as a whole.
   D. Accordance with attestation standards expressing a conclusion about management's assertions.

assess.AICPA.AUD.sup.info-0044

428. When an accountant compiles a client's financial statements accompanied by supplemental information, which of the following is a required element of the accountant's separate report on the supplemental information?

   A. A statement that the information has been compiled from information that is the representation of management without audit or review.
   B. A list of the procedures performed by the accountant during the compilation.
   C. A statement that the accountant did **not** become aware of any material modifications that should be made to the information.
   D. A confirmation of the independence of the accountant with respect to the information presented.

Required Supplementary Information

AICPA.aq.rep.supp.001_17

429. The client's financial reporting includes supplementary financial information outside the basic financial statements but required by the Financial Accounting Standards Board (FASB). Which of the following statements is **correct** regarding the auditor's responsibility for this supplementary financial information?

A. The auditor should perform limited procedures.
B. The auditor should apply tests of details of transactions.
C. The auditor is **not** required to report omissions.
D. The auditor should read the supplementary financial information.

AICPA.090799.AUD-AU

430. What is an auditor's responsibility for supplementary information, such as disclosure of pension information, which is outside the basic financial statements, but required by the GASB?

A. The auditor should engage a specialist, such as an actuary, to verify that management's assertions are reasonable.
B. The auditor's only responsibility for supplementary information is to determine that such information has not been omitted.
C. The auditor should perform tests of transactions to the supplementary information to verify that it is reasonably comparable to the prior year information.
D. The auditor should apply certain limited procedures to the supplementary information and report deficiencies in, or omissions of, such information.

PCAOB on Auditing Supplemental Information

AICPA.140401AUD-SIM

431. The definition of "supplemental information" under PCAOB auditing standards includes all of the following except for

A. A public company's sustainability report consisting of a variety of financial and nonfinancial measures of performance, which is made available to readers on the entity's web site.
B. Supporting schedules that brokers and dealers are required to file with the Securities and Exchange Commission.
C. Information outside of the financial statements that is derived from the entity's accounting records, which is covered by the auditor's report in relation to financial statements audited under PCAOB auditing standards.

D. Information that is required to be presented under the rules of a regulatory authority, which is covered by the auditor's report in relation to financial statements audited under PCAOB auditing standards.

AICPA.140403AUD-SIM

432. The auditor's report on supplemental information under PCAOB auditing standards should include a statement about each of the following except for

A. A statement that the supplemental information is management's responsibility.
B. A statement that the methods of measurement and presentation have not changed from those used in the prior period.
C. A statement that the supplemental information complies with the applicable regulatory requirements.
D. An opinion (or disclaimer) as to whether the supplemental information is fairly stated in relation to the financial statements as a whole.

Alert to Restrict Report

AICPA.130501AUD-SIM

433. When adding an alert to restrict the auditor's report, the auditor should place the alert

A. In the introductory paragraph of the auditor's report.
B. In the Auditor's Responsibility section of the auditor's report.
C. In a paragraph preceding the opinion paragraph.
D. In a paragraph at the end of the auditor's report.

Financial Statements Using Another Country's Framework

AICPA.910549AUD-AU

434. The financial statements of KCP America, a U.S. entity, are prepared for inclusion in the consolidated financial statements of its non-U.S. parent. These financial statements are prepared in conformity with the accounting principles generally accepted in the parent's country and are for use only in that country.

How may KCP America's auditor report on these financial statements?

I. A U.S.-style report (without revision).
II. A U.S.-style report revised to reference the accounting principles of the parent's country.
III. The report form of the parent's country.

	I	II	III
A.	Yes	No	No
B.	No	Yes	No
C.	Yes	No	Yes
D.	No	Yes	Yes

AICPA.941188AUD-AU

435. Before reporting on the financial statements of a U.S. entity that have been prepared in conformity with another country's accounting principles, an auditor practicing in the U.S. should

A. Understand the accounting principles generally accepted in the other country.
B. Be certified by the appropriate auditing or accountancy board of the other country.
C. Notify management that the auditor is required to disclaim an opinion on the financial statements.
D. Receive a waiver from the auditor's state board of accountancy to perform the engagement.

Reporting on Summary Financial Statements

AICPA.911129AUD-AU

436. An auditor may report on condensed financial statements that are derived from complete audited financial statements if the

A. Auditor indicates whether the information in the condensed financial statements is consistent in all material respects.
B. Condensed financial statements are presented in comparative form with the prior year's condensed financial statements.
C. Auditor describes the additional review procedures performed on the condensed financial statements.
D. Condensed financial statements are distributed only to management and the board of directors.

Interim Financial Information

AICPA.090860AUD-SIM

437. Which of the following statements is correct regarding a review of interim financial information under AICPA Professional Standards?

A. The independent accountant should establish an understanding with the client regarding the engagement, but documenting that understanding through a written communication with the client is optional.
B. An engagement to review the entity's interim financial information can only be accepted if the independent accountant has already audited the entity's most recent annual financial statements.
C. The independent accountant should make appropriate inquiries of persons responsible for financial and accounting matters, but need not obtain written representations from management.
D. The independent accountant is required to obtain sufficient knowledge of the entity's business and its internal control related to the interim financial information.

AICPA.111180AUD

438. Which of the following statements would not normally be included in a representation letter for a review of interim financial information?

A. To the best of our knowledge and belief, no events have occurred subsequent to the balance sheet and through the date of this letter that would require adjustment to or disclosure in the interim financial information.
B. We acknowledge our responsibility for the design and implementation of programs and controls to prevent and detect fraud.
C. We understand that a review consists principally of performing analytical procedures and making inquiries about the interim financial information.
D. We have made available to you all financial records and related data.

Other Types of Reports

Reports on Application of Requirements of Framework

AICPA.940567AUD-AU

439. In connection with a proposal to obtain a new client, an accountant in public practice is asked to prepare a written report on the application of accounting principles to a specific transaction.

    The accountant's report should include a statement that

    A. Any difference in the facts, circumstances, or assumptions presented may change the report.
    B. The engagement was performed in accordance with Statements on Standards for Consulting Services.
    C. The guidance provided is for management use only and may not be communicated to the prior or continuing auditors.
    D. Nothing came to the accountant's attention that caused the accountant to believe that the accounting principles violated GAAP.

F/S with Special Purpose Frameworks

AICPA.120733AUD

440. Which of the following items should be included in an auditor's report for financial statements prepared using a special-purpose framework?

    A. A sentence stating that the auditor is responsible for the financial statements.
    B. A title that includes the word "independent."
    C. The signature of the company controller.
    D. A paragraph stating that the audit was conducted in accordance with the special-purpose framework.

AICPA.130722AUD

441. An entity prepares its financial statements on its income tax basis. A description of how that basis differs from GAAP should be included in the

    A. Notes to the financial statements.
    B. Auditor's engagement letter.
    C. Management representation letter.
    D. Introductory paragraph of the auditor's report.

Audits of Single F/S and Specific Elements, Accounts, or Items

AICPA.111184AUD

442. As a condition of obtaining a loan from First National Bank, Maxim Co. is required to submit an audited balance sheet, but not the related statements of income, retained earnings, or cash flows. Maxim would like to engage a CPA to audit only its balance sheet. Under these circumstances, the CPA

    A. May not audit only Maxim's balance sheet if the amount of the loan is material to the financial statements taken as a whole.
    B. May not audit only Maxim's balance sheet if Maxim is a non-issuer.
    C. May audit only Maxim's balance sheet if the CPA disclaims an opinion on the other financial statements.
    D. May audit only Maxim's balance sheet if access to the information underlying the basic financial statements is not limited.

AICPA.120725AUD-SIM

443. An auditor is engaged to report on selected financial data that are included in a client-prepared document containing audited financial statements. Under these circumstances, the report on the selected data should

    A. State that the presentation is based on a special-purpose framework.
    B. Restrict the use of the report to those specified users within the entity.
    C. Refer to the report issued on the entity's audited financial statements.
    D. Indicate that the data are subject to prospective results that may NOT be achieved.

Reporting on Compliance with Requirements in a F/S Audit

AICPA.101088AUD

444. Reports are considered special reports when issued in conjunction with

    A. Interim financial information reviewed to determine whether material modifications should be made to conform with GAAP.
    B. Feasibility studies presented to illustrate an entity's results of operations.
    C. Compliance with aspects of regulatory requirements related to audited financial statements.
    D. Pro forma financial presentations designed to demonstrate the effects of hypothetical transactions.

AICPA.aq.rep.compl.fs.001_18

445. When an audit firm includes a report on compliance with aspects of contractual agreements in the auditor's report on the nonissuer's financial statements, in which paragraph of the audit report should the report on compliance be included?

A. Auditor's responsibility paragraph.
B. Opinion paragraph
C. Other-matter paragraph
D. Emphasis-of-matter paragraph

Service Organizations—User Auditors

AICPA.aq.serv.org.user.002_18

446. Which of the following is a requirement for accepting an attestation engagement to report on the controls at a service organization?

A. The description of the controls is completed prior to the signing of the engagement letter.
B. The service auditor has the competence and capability to perform the engagement.
C. The suitability of the evaluation criteria is reviewed by a third party.
D. Management agrees that the service auditor will be responsible for documenting the controls.

AICPA.130730AUD

447. Which of the following procedures should a user auditor include in the audit plan to create the most efficient audit when an audit client uses a service organization for several processes?

A. Review the service auditor's report on controls placed in operation.
B. Review the service auditor's report and outline the accounting system in a memo to the working papers.
C. Audit the service organization's controls, assess risk, and prepare the audit plan.
D. Audit the service organization's controls to test the work of the service auditor.

Service Organizations—Service Auditors

AICPA.aq.serv.org.serv.001_17

448. A service organization provides processing services for a client's sales orders. Which of the following information is relevant when gathering data for the report on the service organization's internal controls?

A. The client's sales manager reviews accounts receivable balances.
B. The client's data entry clerk used the sales manager's password to make unauthorized changes to customer prices.
C. Credit limits are established and updated by the client's credit department.
D. The service organization's system calculates accounts receivable balances.

AICPA.990530AUD-AU

449. Payroll Data Co. (PDC) processes payroll transactions for a retailer.

Cook, CPA, is engaged to express an opinion on a description of PDC's internal controls placed in operation as of a specific date. These controls are relevant to the retailer's internal control, so Cook's report may be useful in providing the retailer's independent auditor with information necessary to plan a financial statement audit.

Cook's report should

A. Contain a disclaimer of opinion on the operating effectiveness of PDC's controls.
B. State whether PDC's controls were suitably designed to achieve the retailer's objectives.
C. Identify PDC's controls relevant to specific financial statement assertions.
D. Disclose Cook's assessed level of control risk for PDC.

Comfort Letters

AICPA.070636AUD

450. Comfort letters ordinarily are

	Addressed to the Entity's	Signed by the Entity's
A.	Audit committee	Independent auditor
B.	Underwriter of securities	Senior management
C.	Audit committee	Senior management
D.	Underwriter of securities	Independent auditor

AICPA.921158AUD-AU

451. Comfort letters ordinarily are signed by the entity's

A. Independent auditor.
B. Underwriter of securities.
C. Audit committee.
D. Senior management.

Government Auditing Standards

AICPA.aq.gov.aud.stand.001_17

452. A CPA was engaged to audit the financial statements of a municipality that received federal financial assistance and that required a Single Audit for compliance with the terms of the financial assistance. Which of the following guidelines should the CPA consider?

	Generally Accepted Auditing Standards	Government Auditing Standards
A.	Yes	Yes
B.	Yes	No
C.	No	Yes
D.	No	No

AICPA.070634AUD

453. An enterprise engaged a CPA to audit its financial statements in accordance with Government Auditing Standards (the Yellow Book) because of the provisions of government grant funding agreements. Under these circumstances, the CPA is required to report on the enterprise's internal controls either in the report on the financial statements or in

    A. The report on the performance audit.
    B. The notes to the financial statements.
    C. A letter to the government funding agency.
    D. A separate report.

AICPA.101114AUD

454. Which of the following is correct about reporting on compliance with laws and regulations in a financial audit under Government Auditing Standards (the Yellow Book)?

    A. Auditors are not required to report fraud, illegal acts, and other material noncompliance in the audit report.
    B. In some circumstances, auditors are required to report fraud and illegal acts directly to parties external to the audited entity.
    C. The auditor's key findings of the audit of the financial statements should be communicated in a separate report.
    D. The reporting standards in a governmental audit are identical to the auditor's responsibilities under generally accepted auditing standards.

Compliance Audits

AICPA.aq.comp.audits.001_17

455. Before issuing an unmodified report on a compliance audit, an auditor becomes aware of an instance of material noncompliance occurring after the period covered by the audit. The **least** appropriate response by the auditor would be to

    A. Discuss the matter with management and, if appropriate, those charged with governance.
    B. Issue a qualified compliance report describing the subsequent noncompliance.
    C. Determine whether the noncompliance relates to conditions that existed as of period end or arose subsequent to the reporting period.
    D. Modify the standard compliance report to include a paragraph describing the nature of the subsequent noncompliance.

AICPA.101090AUD

456. How does Office of Management and Budget Circular A-133, *Audits of States, Local Governments, and Non-Profit Organizations*, define a subrecipient?

    A. As a nonfederal entity that provides a federal award to another entity to carry out a federal program.
    B. As an individual who receives and expends federal awards received from a pass-through entity
    C. As a dealer, distributor, merchant, or other seller providing goods or services that are required for the conduct of a federal program
    D. As a nonfederal entity that expends federal awards received from another entity to carry out a federal program

SSARSs—General Principles

AICPA.151002AUD-SIM

457. Unconditional requirements in the clarified Statements on Standards for Accounting and Review Services are indicated by the word

    A. Should.
    B. Must.
    C. May.
    D. Could.

AICPA.931112AUD-AU

458. A CPA is required to comply with the provisions of Statements on Standards for Accounting and Review Services when

	Processing Financial Data for Clients of Other CPA Firms	Consulting on Accounting Matters
A.	Yes	Yes
B.	Yes	No
C.	No	Yes
D.	No	No

SSARSs—Preparation of Financial Statements

AICPA.151005AUD-SIM

459. The clarified SSARSs applicable to preparation engagements (AR-C 70) do not apply to the following engagements, except for

A. Preparing financial statements to be presented alongside a personal financial plan.
B. Preparing financial statements for submission to taxing authorities.
C. Preparing financial statement in connection with litigation services.
D. Assisting with preparing financial statements by performing bookkeeping services.

SSARSs—Compilation Engagements

AICPA.aq.ssarss.comp.002_17

460. If prior-period compiled financial statements have been restated and the predecessor accounting firm decides **not** to reissue its report, the successor accounting firm

A. May be engaged to reissue the prior-period report.
B. May **not** be engaged to reissue the prior-period report.
C. Must disclose the prior-period misstatements in the introductory paragraph of its current-year report.
D. Must issue a combined report of both the prior-period and current-period financial statements.

AICPA.111188AUD

461. General Retailing, a nonissuer, has asked Ford, CPA, to compile its financial statements that omit substantially all disclosures required by GAAP. Ford may comply with General's request provided the omission is clearly indicated in Ford's report and the

A. Distribution of the financial statements and Ford's report is restricted to internal use only.
B. Reason for omitting the disclosures is acknowledged in the notes to the financial statements.
C. Omitted disclosures would not influence any potential creditor's conclusions about General's financial position.
D. Omission is not undertaken with the intention of misleading the users of General's financial statements.

AICPA.130719AUD

462. Which of the following would **not** be included in an accountant's documentation of a compilation of a client's financial statements?

A. Discussion with the client regarding the proper presentation of gross cash flows for investment purchases.
B. An engagement letter.
C. A memo to the CFO about a potentially significant fraud revealed during compilation procedures.
D. A review of the segregation of duties in the cash disbursement process.

SSARSs—Review Engagements

AICPA.aq.ssarss.review.002_18

463. If an accountant is performing a review engagement for a nonissuer and considers it necessary to communicate a matter that is not presented in the financial statements, then the accountant should include this information in which of the following paragraphs in the review report?

A. The opinion paragraph.
B. The introductory paragraph
C. The other-matter paragraph
D. The emphasis-of-matter paragraph

AICPA.aq.ssarss.review.001_17

464. During a review of financial statements, an accountant decides to emphasize a matter in the review report. Which of the following is an example of a matter that the accountant would *most likely* want to emphasize?

A. Other entities in the same industry have recently changed from LIFO to FIFO.
B. The IRS has notified the entity that it intends to audit income tax returns for prior years.
C. The entity has had significant transactions with related parties.
D. The entity has had significant tax expenses as a result of a new tax law.

AICPA.111169AUD

465. A CPA started to audit the financial statements of a nonissuer. After completing certain audit procedures, the client requested the CPA to change the engagement to a review because of a scope limitation. The CPA concludes that there is reasonable justification for the change. Under these circumstances, the CPA's review report should include a

A. Statement that a review is substantially less in scope than an audit.
B. Reference to the scope limitation that caused the changed engagement.
C. Description of the auditing procedures that were completed before the engagement was changed.
D. Reference to the CPA's justification for agreeing to change the engagement.

AICPA.120736AUD

466. Which of the following procedures would be generally performed when evaluating the accounts receivable balance in an engagement to review financial statements in accordance with *Statements on Standards for Accounting and Review Services*?

A. Perform a reasonableness test of the balance by computing days' sales in receivables.
B. Vouch a sample of subsequent cash receipts from customers.
C. Confirm individually significant receivable balances with customers.
D. Review subsequent bank statements for evidence of cash deposits.

SSARSs—Other Topics

AICPA.111168AUD

467. A CPA is reporting on comparative financial statements of a nonissuer. The CPA audited the prior year's financial statements and reviewed those of the current year in accordance with *Statements on Standards for Accounting and Review Services* (SSARS). The CPA has added a separate paragraph to the review report to describe the responsibility assumed for the prior year's audited financial statements. This separate paragraph should indicate

A. The type of opinion expressed previously.
B. That the CPA did **not** update the assessment of control risk.

C. The reasons for the change from an audit to a review.
D. That the audit report should **no** longer be relied on.

AICPA.111201AUD

468. An accountant has been engaged to compile pro forma financial statements. During the accountant's acceptance procedures, it is discovered that the accountant is not independent with respect to the company. What action should the accountant take with regard to the compilation?

A. The accountant should discuss the lack of independence with legal counsel to determine whether it is appropriate to accept the engagement.
B. The accountant should disclose the lack of independence in the accountant's compilation report.
C. The accountant should withdraw from the engagement.
D. The accountant should compile the pro forma financial statements but should not provide a compilation report.

AICPA.941179AUD-AU

469. Gole, CPA, is engaged to review the 20x2 financial statements of North Co., a nonpublic entity. Previously, Gole audited North's 20x1 financial statements and expressed an unmodified opinion. Gole decides to include a separate paragraph in the 20x2 review report because North plans to present comparative financial statements for 20x2 and 20x1.

This separate paragraph should indicate that

A. The 20x2 review report is intended solely for the information of management and the board of directors.
B. The 20x1 auditor's report may no longer be relied on.
C. No auditing procedures were performed after the date of the 20x1 auditor's report.
D. There are justifiable reasons for changing the level of service from an audit to a review.

Other Professional Services

AICPA on Reporting on Internal Control in an Integrated Audit

assess.AICPA.AUD.aud.rep-0045

470. Which of the following best describes the earliest date for an auditor's report?

A. The last day of audit fieldwork.
B. The date all audit procedures have been completed and the audit file has been assembled.
C. The date audit documentation was completed.
D. The date the auditor has obtained sufficient appropriate audit evidence to support the opinion.

assess.AICPA.AUD.rep.ic.audit-0033

471. Which of the following statements correctly describes the "top-down approach" used during an audit of internal control over financial reporting?

A. Begin reviewing balance sheet accounts and then review income statement accounts.
B. Begin reviewing income statement accounts and then review balance sheet accounts.
C. Begin by understanding the overall risks to internal control over financial reporting at the financial statement level.
D. Begin by understanding the overall risks to internal control over financial reporting at the general ledger level.

PCAOB on Reporting on Internal Control in an Integrated Audit

AICPA.111179AUD

472. Each of the following types of controls is considered to be an entity-level control, except those

A. Relating to the control environment.
B. Pertaining to the company's risk assessment process.
C. Regarding the company's annual stockholder meeting.
D. Addressing policies over significant risk management practices.

AICPA08115017.AUD.SOA.5

473. According to PCAOB auditing standards, when the auditor issues separate reports on the financial statements and on internal control over financial reporting,

A. The reports will normally have different dates, depending upon when audit fieldwork is completed for the financial statements and when the tests of control are completed.
B. Each report should be entitled "Report of Independent Auditor."
C. Each report should include a separate paragraph that discusses the "inherent limitations" of any audit engagement.
D. Each report should include a paragraph that references the other related report.

PCAOB on Reporting Whether Previously Reported Material Weakness Continues to Exist

AICPA08115001.AUD.SOA.6

474. PCAOB auditing standards apply when an issuer's auditor is engaged to report on whether a previously reported material weakness in internal control over financial reporting continues to exist as of a date specified by management. Which of the following statements is correct?

A. Whenever an auditor's report on internal control over financial reporting identifies a material weakness, the auditor must also be engaged to issue a subsequent report within three months to indicate whether the previously reported material weakness continues to exist.
B. Whenever an auditor's report on internal control over financial reporting identifies a material weakness, the auditor must also be engaged to issue a subsequent report within six months to indicate whether the previously reported material weakness continues to exist.
C. Whenever an auditor's report on internal control over financial reporting identifies a material weakness, the auditor must also be engaged to issue a subsequent report within nine months to indicate whether the previously reported material weakness continues to exist.
D. PCAOB auditing standards do not require an auditor to report whether a previously reported material weakness continues to exist, so such an engagement is voluntary.

AICPA08115001.AUD.SOA.8

475. According to PCAOB auditing standards, in evaluating whether a material weakness exists, an auditor should focus on materiality at the

   A. Individual account-balance level.
   B. Financial statement level.
   C. Planning-stage level.
   D. Quantitative level without regard to the qualitative circumstances.

Auditing Employee Benefit Plans

aq.aud.emp.001_2017

476. Which legislation is most directly associated with pension and welfare plans?

   A. Uniform Commercial Code of 1952.
   B. Securities Act of 1933
   C. Employee Retirement Income Security Act of 1974
   D. Sarbanes-Oxley Act of 2002

aq.aud.emp.011_2017

477. Which financial statement is specifically mentioned in the first paragraph of the auditor's report on an employee benefit plan's comparative financial statements?

   A. Statements of financial position.
   B. Statements of net assets available for benefits.
   C. Statements of investment income and its allocation to participants.
   D. Statements of participants' equity in plan assets.

Introduction to Attestation Standards

AICPA.aq.attest.stand.001_17

478. Which of the following services provides the **least** assurance regarding the fairness of financial statements?

   A. Review.
   B. Audit.
   C. Compilation.
   D. Attestation.

AICPA.130728AUD

479. A practitioner is engaged to express an opinion on management's assertion that the square footage of a warehouse offered for sale is 150,000 square feet. The practitioner should refer to which of the following sources for professional guidance?

   A. *Statements on Auditing Standards.*
   B. *Statements on Standards for Attestation Engagements.*
   C. *Statements on Standards for Accounting and Review Services.*
   D. *Statements on Standards for Consulting Services.*

Attestation Standards—Common Concepts

AICPA.120737AUD

480. According to the AICPA *Statements on Standards for Attestation Engagements*, a public accounting firm should establish quality control policies to provide assurance about which of the following matters related to agreed-upon procedures engagements?

   A. Use of the report is NOT restricted.
   B. The public accounting firm takes responsibility for the sufficiency of procedures.
   C. The practitioner is independent from the client and other specified parties.
   D. The practitioner sets the criteria to be used in the determination of findings.

Examination Engagements

aq.exam.engage.001_2017

481. An engagement letter for an examination should address all of the following matters, except for

   A. The objective and scope of the examination engagement.
   B. The dollar amount associated with the practitioner's materiality threshold.
   C. A statement about the inherent limitations of an examination engagement.
   D. A statement that identifies the criteria for measurement or evaluation of the subject matter involved.

AICPA.070617AUD

482. A CPA is engaged to examine management's assertion that the entity's schedule of investment returns is presented in accordance with specific criteria. In performing this engagement, the CPA should comply with the provisions of

   A. Statements on Standards for Accounting and Review Services (SSARS.
   B. Statements on Auditing Standards (SAS).
   C. Statements on Standards for Consulting Services (SSCS).
   D. Statements on Standards for Attestation Engagements (SSAE).

Examination Reports

aq.exam.report.001_2017

483. When the practitioner determines that the subject matter of an examination engagement has a misstatement that is both material and pervasive, the practitioner should express a (an)

    A. Unmodified opinion with an explanatory paragraph.
    B. Disclaimer of opinion.
    C. Adverse opinion.
    D. Qualified opinion.

aq.exam.report.002_2017

484. When the practitioner determines that the subject matter of an examination engagement is materially misstated, but that the misstatement is not pervasive, the practitioner should express a (an)

    A. Qualified opinion either directly on the subject matter or on the responsible party's assertion when the assertion acknowledges the misstatement.
    B. Qualified opinion directly on the subject matter.
    C. Qualified opinion on the responsible party's assertion, whether or not the assertion acknowledges the misstatement.
    D. Adverse opinion on either the responsible party's assertion or directly on the subject matter.

Review Engagements

aq.review.engage.001_2017

485. What should the practitioner do when the responsible party (who is also the engaging party) declines to provide a written assertion for a review engagement?

    A. Withdraw from the engagement when that is permitted by applicable law.
    B. Disclose that refusal in the practitioner's review report.
    C. Modify the review report to express a qualified conclusion.
    D. Modify the engagement letter to state that a written assertion will not be provided.

aq.review.engage.002_2017

486. What should the practitioner do when the responsible party (who is also the engaging party) declines to provide the requested written representations for a review engagement?

    A. Withdraw from the engagement when that is permitted by applicable law.

    B. Disclose that refusal in the practitioner's review report
    C. Modify the review report to express an adverse conclusion
    D. Attempt to obtain satisfactory oral responses from the responsible party

Review Reports

aq.review.report.001_2017

487. Which of the following statements about a practitioner's review report for an attestation engagement is correct?

    A. The Statements on Standards for Attestation Engagements require CPAs to express a review report in a standardized format.
    B. The practitioner should report on the responsible party's written assertion, not directly on the subject matter.
    C. The practitioner's review report should include a disclaimer of opinion.
    D. When the subject matter of a review engagement has a misstatement that is material but not pervasive, the practitioner should restrict the distribution of the report to the engaging party.

aq.review.report.002_2017

488. The practitioner's review report for an attestation engagement should include a restricted-use paragraph in all of the following circumstances, **except** for

    A. When the criteria used to evaluate the subject matter are available only to certain parties.
    B. When the engaging party is not the responsible party and the responsible party declines to provide the requested written representations but does provide satisfactory oral responses to the practitioner.
    C. When the practitioner refers to an external specialist because the practitioner's conclusion is modified and reference to the specialist may be helpful to readers in understanding the reason for the modification.
    D. When the criteria used to evaluate the subject matter are appropriate only for a limited number of parties.

Agreed-Upon Procedures Engagements

AICPA.aq.agreed.proced.001_17

489. A practitioner's report on agreed-upon procedures should contain which of the following statements?

 A. The procedures performed were those agreed to by the specified parties identified in the report.
 B. Sufficiency of procedures is the responsibility of the practitioner.
 C. All classification codes appeared to comply with such performance documents.
 D. Nothing came to my attention as a result of applying the procedures.

AICPA.130708AUD

490. Which of the following should a practitioner perform as part of an engagement for agreed-upon procedures in accordance with *Statements on Standards for Attestation Engagements*?

 A. Issue a report on findings based on specified procedures performed.
 B. Assess whether the procedures meet the needs of the parties.
 C. Express negative assurance on findings of work performed.
 D. Report the differences between agreed-upon and audit procedures.

Prospective Information

AICPA.aq.fin.forecasts.001_17

491. In which of the following situations will a practitioner disclaim an opinion on an examination of prospective financial statements?

 A. The prospective financial statements depart from AICPA presentation guidelines.
 B. The practitioner was **not** able to perform certain procedures deemed necessary.
 C. The prospective financial statements fail to disclose significant assumptions.
 D. The significant assumptions do **not** provide a reasonable basis for the statements.

assess.AICPA.AUD.fin.forecasts-0008

492. A company hired a practitioner to perform an examination of prospective financial statements. The practitioner concluded that the assumptions did not provide a reasonable basis for the prospective financial statements. Which of the following types of opinion should the practitioner issue?

 A. Unqualified.
 B. Qualified.
 C. Adverse.
 D. Disclaimer.

Pro Forma Financial Information

AICPA.940568AUD-AU

493. An accountant's report on a review of pro forma financial information should include a

 A. Statement that the entity's internal control structure was not relied on in the review.
 B. Disclaimer of opinion on the financial statements from which the pro forma financial information is derived.
 C. Caveat that it is uncertain whether the transaction or event reflected in the pro forma financial information will ever occur.
 D. Reference to the financial statements from which the historical financial information is derived.

assess.AICPA.AUD.pro.forma.fin-0003

494. A practitioner reporting on pro forma financial information does **not** possess an understanding of the client's business and the industry in which the client operates. The practitioner should take which of the following actions?

 A. Issue a disclaimer, because the scope of work was **not** sufficient to express an opinion.
 B. Review industry trade journals.
 C. Refer a substantial portion of the audit to another CPA who will act as the principal. practitioner.
 D. Perform ratio analysis of the financial data of comparable prior periods.

Compliance Attestation

AICPA.aq.comp.attest.001_17

495. An independent auditor is issuing an audit report for a governmental entity and plans to issue separate reports on internal control over financial reporting and compliance with laws and regulations. The auditor should do which of the following?

 A. Report to the governing authority that separate reports will be issued.
 B. Issue the same opinion in each report.
 C. State in the audit report that separate reports will be issued.
 D. Obtain permission from the audit committee to issue separate reports.

AICPA.010413AUD-AU

496. Mill, CPA, was engaged by a group of royalty recipients to apply agreed-upon procedures to financial data supplied by Modern Co. regarding Modern's written assertion about its compliance with contractual requirements to pay royalties.

Mill's report on these agreed-upon procedures should contain a (an)

A. Disclaimer of opinion about the fair presentation of Modern's financial statements.
B. List of the procedures performed (or reference thereto) and Mill's findings.
C. Opinion about the effectiveness of Modern's internal control activities concerning royalty payments.
D. Acknowledgment that the sufficiency of the procedures is solely Mill's responsibility.

Management's Discussion and Analysis (MD&A)

AICPA.020413AUD-AU

497. A CPA is required to comply with the provisions of Statements on Standards for Attestation Engagements (SSAE) when engaged to

A. Report on financial statements that the CPA generated through the use of computer software.
B. Review management's discussion and analysis (MD&A) prepared pursuant to rules and regulations adopted by the SEC.
C. Provide the client with a financial statement format that does not include dollar amounts.
D. Audit financial statements that the client prepared for use in another country.

testbank.REPT-0116

498. Which of the following forms of auditor association are possible relating to management's discussion and analysis (MD&A)?

	Review	Examination
A.	Yes	No
B.	Yes	Yes
C.	No	Yes
D.	No	No

testbank.REPT-0117

499. Which of the following is not an assertion embodied in management's discussion and analysis (MD&A)?

A. Completeness.
B. Consistency with the financial statements.
C. Occurrence.
D. Rights and obligations.

Assurance Services

AICPA.990402AUD-AU

500. Which of the following is a term for an attest engagement in which a CPA assesses a client's commercial Internet site for predefined criteria that are designed to measure transaction integrity, information protection, and disclosure of business practices?

A. ElectroNet.
B. EDIFACT.
C. TechSafe.
D. WebTrust.

Answers and Explanations

1. **Answer: A**

   A member serving in multiple roles should choose the most restrictive applicable provisions and that will be the standards applying to MIPPs.

2. **Answer: B**

   The code requires members to cooperate with each other to improve the art of accounting (and to maintain the public's confidence in the profession, and to carry out the profession's special responsibilities).

3. **Answer: A**

   Ethical standards are not legally required, and so the goal in creating them lies in showing a willingness to go above and beyond minimum requirements. Observing ethical standards shows the public that CPAs are more concerned than are most professions with working in an ethical and trustworthy fashion.

4. **Answer: C**

   Unusual danger is not part of the Conceptual Framework.

5. **Answer: D**

   Because the three chocies provided are all examples of sources of safeguards, this is the best answer.

6. **Answer: D**

   Because the seller has not been a client for at least ten years, it seems unlikely that there could be a conflict of interest here. Only if the accounting firm had learned some confidential proprietary information while serving the client that is still of value a decade later would there be some sort of a conflict here.

7. **Answer: D**

   Because the three choices provided are all examples of conflicts of interest, this is the best answer.

8. **Answer: D**

   Because all three answer choices provided are correct, this is the best answer. Maria should also be very concerned about gifts from ABC's directors.

9. **Answer: A**

   At this stage, Son should keep things in-house. The AICPA rules recommend that he go to the "appropriate level of management," such as his supervisor's superior, the client's audit committee, etc. However, if that does not produce satisfaction and Son is convinced that the financials are about to be materially misstated, he should consider resigning and contacting regulatory authorities.

10. **Answer: C**

    Communication is critical in determining the responsibilities of auditors when they have disagreements with their superiors over serious matters.

11. **Answer: D**

    Because the answers provided are all correct, this is the best answer.

12. **Answer: D**

    Because choices II and III are both accurate, this is the best answer.

13. **Answer: B**

    The AICPA and state accountancy boards do not expect CPAs to be "Ms. or Mr. Super Accountant."

14. **Answer: A**

    Material departures from GAAP, which require material modifications, violate the Code of Professional Conduct.

15. **Answer: C**

    The outsourcing of professional services requires notification and client approval.

16. **Answer: B**

    Members may advocate on behalf of tax and advisory service clients, although they should never stretch the bounds of performance standards, go beyond sound and reasonable professional practice, or compromise their credibility.

17. **Answer: D**

    All of these are listed as discreditable acts according to the Acts Discreditable Rule. This is the best answer.

18. **Answer: B**

    While the SEC and most government agencies oppose full indemnification of wrongdoers, contribution is typically allowed and, therefore, would not violate the Code.

19. **Answer: A**

    Spinner may, under proper circumstances, have to convey to Lasco (a) client-provided records, (b) client records prepared by Spinner, and (c) supporting records. However, it should not have to convey its audit documentation, which it owns.

20. **Answer: D**

    Client records belong to the client and should be returned to the client upon demand (even if there is an ongoing fee dispute).

21. **Answer: C**

    Only audit documentation may be retained indefinitely by a CPA. Such documentation may be necessary for defending against a malpractice suit. Client records, however, must be returned to a client upon request.

22. **Answer: D**

    Assuming that Harriett is not also an audit client, then commissions and referral fees are permitted, if properly disclosed.

23. **Answer: C**

    Because both I and II are accurate, this is the best answer.

24. **Answer: B**

    Tax accountants can accept referral fees and commissions. However, they should be disclosed to the client (and the question instructs us to assume appropriate disclosure).

25. **Answer: D**

    While auditors may not receive contingent fees for performing attest-related services, seeking a private letter ruling is not an attest-related service. Unless the auditor is also providing attest services for the client, a contingent fee for seeking a private letter ruling is allowed.

26. **Answer: B**

    Because during an examination the IRS will almost certainly look at the merits of the tax return, there is no temptation to play the "audit lottery," so contingent fees are allowed under the Code. Of course, in regard to attest clients, PCAOB rules say that an auditor of a public company may not provide to it *any* tax services on a contingent fee basis and remain independent.

27. **Answer: C**

    This is the best answer, as this question emphasizes the importance of the confidentiality duty that accountants have vis-a-vis all their clients.

28. **Answer: A**

    It is extremely unlikely that a client's mail clerk would have authority to approve the release of confidential financial information. The CPA, therefore, should not release it.

29. **Answer: B**

    A CPA should refuse to produce confidential client records in response to a mere request from the IRS or SEC.

30. **Answer: B**

    There are only a few circumstances in which information may be disclosed without the consent of the client. These include when a valid court order demanding release of the information is issued, when a quality review board of a state's CPA society requests the information, when a client consents to disclosure, and whenever professional obligations otherwise require it.

31. **Answer: B**

    Disclosure may not be made to any party without either a court order or the consent of the client, unless the requesting party is a state CPA regulatory body. If the client consents, then the information may be released to anyone that the client has approved.

32. **Answer: D**

    Because the three choices provided are all accurate, this is the best answer. Accounting firms have substantial leeway in choosing names, so long as they do not mislead.

33. **Answer: D**

    Because all three choices are all permitted, this is the best answer.

34. **Answer: A**

    Attest firms must be majority owned by CPAs.

35. **Answer: A**

    As CEO, Dort would be a PTI, as she would oversee, even if only indirectly, the work of the audit team for RTDI.

36. **Answer: D**

    Because the three choices are all accurate, this is the best answer.

37. **Answer: C**

    As a staff member who works on the engagement, Bit is a "covered member."

38. **Answer: D**

    Firing these employees is not required and would not truly advance the cause of independence.

39. **Answer: A**

    Independence is required if use of such reports is unrestricted.

40. **Answer: D**

    Because all three answer choices are correct, this is the best answer.

41. **Answer: C**

    It is proper for an engagement letter to require an attest client to indemnify an audit firm for liability and costs resulting from knowing misrepresentations by the client's management.

42. **Answer: B**

    The code does note that entering into binding arbitration potentially creates independence problems by placing the firm and the client in positions of material adverse interests, creating a self-interest threat.

43. **Answer: A**

    A member in public practice may not sign a current-year audit report if it has unpaid fees from the client for services provided more than one year prior.

44. **Answer: D**

    Lil need not resign from her firm…there is plenty of work that she can do for other clients.

45. **Answer: D**

    Because JKL is agent-managed, it is akin to a limited partnership and absent evidence to the contrary we presume that Sam's interest is passive. Therefore, this investment is viewed as indirect.

46. **Answer: D**

    This is a direct financial interest. Therefore, materiality is not a factor. A direct financial interest impairs independence even if it is immaterial.

47. **Answer: A**

    There would be an impairment here, for Jo owns a direct though immaterial interest in the audit client: the mutual fund.

48. **Answer: C**

    Both of these situations create an independence problem. The ability of Sally and Joe to self-direct their investments makes their interests in ABC direct. Therefore, there is an independence problem even if the investments are immaterial.

49. **Answer: D**

    Unless Art participates in the investment decisions of his limited liability corporation, which is not indicated in the facts, his interests in its underlying investments are indirect if the LLC is agent managed.

50. **Answer: D**

    Because all three situations create independence problems, this is the best answer.

51. **Answer: D**

    This statement is true—these are the two things that Spencer must ensure in order to maintain this account while being a covered member.

52. **Answer: D**

    Because the three answer choices provided are all incorrect, this is the best answer.

53. **Answer: B**

    Under these facts, Kim's interest in ABC is a direct financial interest, which creates an independence problem.

54. **Answer: A**

    Covered members and attest clients may both own the stock of a widely-held public corporation.

55. **Answer: D**

    This would not be a problem given that Lynn chose not to ask for the loan. Had she actually borrowed the money, there would obviously have been an independence problem.

56. **Answer: D**

    Because Tondry only has a minority share in the business, even though the business provides services to an attest client, there is no independence violation and no need for the business' employees to follow independence requirements.

    When the member, individually or collectively with the member's firm or others in the firm, does not control the separate business, the provisions of the code would apply to the member's actions but not t o the separate business, its other (nonmember) owners, and its professional employees. For example, the separate business could enter into a contingent fee arrangement with the member's attest client or accept commissions for the referral of products or services to the member's attest client.

57. **Answer: B**

    If an operating lease is on normal terms and all amounts are paid in accordance with the terms of the lease, there are no independence problems.

58. **Answer: A**

    Because Microsoft is a public company, this situation creates no independence problem, although it might be considered a joint investment.

59. **Answer: D**

    This statement is not true. An IFM of a covered member is not completely barred from holding a material indirect interest in an audit client.

However, three safeguards must be met: (1) the covered member (Wiley) may not be on the attest team or be in a position to influence the team; (2) the investment in BMC must be an unavoidable consequence of Karen's participation in her employer's plan; and (3) if Karen is given an opportunity to take another plan option and divest her interest in BMC, she must do so.

60. **Answer: B**

    Betsy is in a position to influence the attest engagement team. Her live-in lover is a spousal equivalent, which qualifies him as an immediate family member. He is therefore covered by the independence rules. Although he could hold a non-key position, if he owns enough AAD stock that it is material to him, there is clearly a significant independence problem.

61. **Answer: C**

    Immediate family members include spouses, spousal equivalents, and dependents but not nondependent children.

62. **Answer: B**

    Close relatives include parents, siblings, and nondependent children but not spousal equivalents, who are immediate family members.

63. **Answer: D**

    The role of advisor to a client's board is not forbidden by AICPA independence rules.

64. **Answer: D**

    This is the best answer. The SOX provision addresses CEOs, controllers, CFOs, CAOs, or persons serving in equivalent positions.

65. **Answer: A**

    The cooling-off period is one year, so this answer is correct.

66. **Answer: D**

    This is false. Independence would not be impaired by this gift which seems to be clearly insignificant (only $100) to Solly. Additionally, the limitation on gifts applies only to the firm, audit team members and PTIs. It does not apply to an OPIO like Solly, though the Conceptual

Framework is always lurking in the background and should be considered just to be safe.

67. **Answer: D**

Because the three answer choices provided are all correct, this is the best answer.

68. **Answer: A**

Regarding independence, the firm, team members, and those in a position to influence may not accept gifts from attest clients unless the value of those gifts is clearly insignificant to the recipient.

69. **Answer: C**

The activity described sounds like typical human relations consulting where the final decision as to whom to hire is made by the client.

70. **Answer: D**

This choice is **not** true. If Pilden takes the proper steps (avoids management responsibilities, induces Dimsdale to assume such responsibilities and to oversee the NAS, documents its understanding in writing, etc.), then Pilden may attend board meetings as a nonvoting advisor.

71. **Answer: D**

Because the other three answer choices are all examples of "management responsibilities," this is the best answer.

72. **Answer: D**

Because the other three answer choices are all examples of communications that are not deemed nonaudit services, this is the best answer.

73. **Answer: B**

Sarbanes-Oxley requires audit committee preapproval.

74. **Answer: D**

Harvey is hosting the attest client's records on its behalf, and this presents a management participation threat to independence. Harvey may hold the original records to help prepare the tax returns but should return them when the engagement is completed (or annually if the engagement is multiyear).

75. **Answer: D**

This is a management responsibility that goes too far to avoid an independence problem.

76. **Answer: B**

This is merely an advisory function and is permissible.

77. **Answer: A**

This gift is reasonable under the circumstances of Jessie's birthday and threatens neither objectivity nor integrity.

78. **Answer: D**

This is not true—this is a problem for members in public practice who may not be able to be adequate watchdogs of attest clients if they become too familiar with them. But no compliance threat arises for a member in business who works for an employer for a long time.

79. **Answer: D**

Because the three choices provided are all examples of "other members," this is the best answer.

80. **Answer: D**

Because the three choices provided are all examples of discreditable acts, this is the best answer.

81. **Answer: B**

Even other members must avoid discreditable acts.

82. **Answer: C**

Tom has disassociated from Weasel by severing all ties and has served the one-year cooling-off period.

83. **Answer: A**

Tina is both a CFM and an Immediate Family Member (IFM) if we assume that she is dependent on her mother, which she probably is.

84. **Answer: D**

This relationship is permissible so long as Kim has no authority to make investment decisions for the trust.

85. **Answer: D**

    All answer choices impair independence under SEC rules.

86. **Answer: D**

    This is permitted. Mary doesn't seem to be a covered person. Even if she were, this loan would be permitted so long as, and this appears to be the case, VWX is a financial institution, the loan is fully collateralized, and normal lending procedures were followed.

87. **Answer: C**

    Auditors of public companies cannot provide any services to an audit client on a contingent fee basis.

88. **Answer: A**

    In each of these three cases, the accounting firm is to describe in writing important issues surrounding the relationship, discuss those specifically with the audit committee, and document the discussion for posterity.

89. **Answer: B**

    Because Omar is in a Financial Reporting Oversight Role and none of the exceptions appears to apply, he may not receive any tax services from Single.

90. **Answer: D**

    A government internal audit function is presumed to be free from organizational independence impairments for reporting internally when the head of the organization is removed from political pressures to conduct audits objectively, without fear of political reprisal.

91. **Answer: A**

    Developing program policies for an audited entity would impair auditor independence. This is one of many management roles that, under GAO rules, an auditor may not perform for an audited entity without impairing independence.

92. **Answer: B**

    The potential impairment threat is external, stemming from the threatened firing.

93. **Answer: C**

    Under GAGAS, auditors should never audit their own work, which is what is happening here. This creates an independence problem so severe that it cannot be remedied by application of supplemental safeguards.

94. **Answer: C**

    This is a government entity, and no doubt an entity that receives federal funds, so in addition to the AICPA's Code of Professional Conduct, GAGAS and attendant independence rules will apply.

95. **Answer: D**

    Choices A and C would both be correct under the current AICPA Code of Professional Conduct as well, although B would not. But B is correct under DOL standards.

96. **Answer: D**

    Because all three of the initial choices (A, B, and C) are correct, the best answer is D.

97. **Answer: A**

    Under DOL guidelines, many consulting services are permitted, but one cannot maintain independence while auditing records that one maintained in the first place.

98. **Answer: B**

    Department of Labor rules allow audit firms to provide actuarial services to a plan without impairing independence.

99. **Answer: C**

    The auditor's primary role is to provide an impartial (independent) report on the reliability of management's financial statements. These financial statements are distributed to interested parties outside of the reporting entity itself, such as actual or potential shareholders and creditors, major customers and suppliers, employees, regulators, and others for their decision-making (resource allocation) needs. Management prepares the financial statements and represents that they are in fact fairly presented while the auditor is auditing such representations.

100. **Answer: A**

    GAAS requires the auditor to obtain "sufficient appropriate audit evidence..."

101. **Answer: B**

GAAS requires auditors to have adequate technical training and proficiency in auditing.

102. **Answer: B**

The exercise of due professional care requires that a critical review of the work completed and the judgments made be performed at every level of supervision.

103. **Answer: B**

Articles in the *Journal of Accountancy* have no authoritative status, and would be classified as *other auditing publications*.

104. **Answer: C**

The word *should* indicates a presumptively mandatory requirement.

105. **Answer: D**

The AICPA's quality control standards are applicable to the CPA firm's portfolio of audit (and other financial statement related) services, which is consistent with this answer.

106. **Answer: B**

A firm is required to establish an appropriate system of quality control to provide reasonable assurance of conforming with professional standards.

107. **Answer: A**

A firm establishes a system of internal control in order to provide reasonable assurance that the professional services provided will conform to professional standards.

108. **Answer: B**

Differences of opinion between the engagement partner and the quality control reviewer should be resolved using the firm's established policies and procedures.

109. **Answer: C**

Substantive evidential matter required by the Principles may include evidence obtained through the performance of substantive analytical procedures (as well as that obtained through inspection, observation, inquiries, and confirmation). Analytical procedures performed as substantive tests can be used to provide substantive evidential matter.

110. **Answer: B**

The audit work performed by each assistant should be reviewed for adequacy and to ensure that it supports the conclusions reached.

111. **Answer: B**

The second sentence of the Auditor's Responsibility section states as follows: "We conducted our audits in accordance with auditing standards generally accepted in the United States of America."

112. **Answer: A**

The objective of the requirement is to prevent misinterpretations regarding the degree of responsibility the auditor is assuming when his name is associated with financial statements.

113. **Answer: D**

The standard auditor's report on comparative financial statements states explicitly that evidence is obtained (and therefore examined) and implies that accounting principles have been consistently applied. Such application is assumed unless the report indicates otherwise.

114. **Answer: B**

GAAS require an auditor to express an opinion on the financial statements. That responsibility is EXPLICITLY represented in the Auditor's Responsibility paragraphs of the auditor's unmodified report which states that the auditor's responsibility is to express an opinion.

115. **Answer: A**

An attestation engagement is one in which the practitioner is engaged to issue an examination, a review, or an agreed-upon procedures report on subject matter or an assertion about subject matter that is the responsibility of another party.

116. **Answer: B**

The type of engagement described is a WebTrust assurance engagement. It is performed in accordance with the Statements on Standards for Attestation Engagements.

117. **Answer: A**

The FASB establishes accounting standards. PCAOB establishes auditing standards.

118. **Answer: C**

The PCAOB is a standard-setting body for certain matters related to registered public accounting firms (including auditing and quality control, among other matters). However, the PCAOB is not an accounting standard-setting body and does not promulgate GAAP affecting the financial statements of issuers.

119. **Answer: B**

Title II of the Sarbanes-Oxley Act of 2002 establishes 5 years as the upper limit for how long someone can serve as the engagement partner or review partner before mandatory rotation is required.

120. **Answer: C**

Registered public accounting firms that audit more than 100 issuers must be inspected annually; those that audit 100 or fewer issuers must be inspected every three years. In this case, a registered public accounting firm that issues audit report to 50 issuers would be inspected every three years.

121. **Answer: D**

By process of elimination, this answer is not identified by PCAOB auditing standards as a matter that is required documentation in an engagement quality review. There is no expectation that fraud issues will be routinely identified by the audit team, nor does the quality reviewer provide a separate assessment of such matters.

122. **Answer: A**

The PCAOB (specifically, AS Section 1220) identifies the following as "significant engagement deficiencies": when (1) the engagement team failed to obtain sufficient appropriate evidence; (2) the engagement team reached an inappropriate overall conclusion; (3) the engagement report is not appropriate; or (4) the firm is not independent of its client. Since B, C, and D are specifically identified as significant engagement deficiencies, A is the correct answer. If management's accounting estimates are unreasonable, it constitutes a GAAP

departure, not a deficiency in the performance of the audit engagement.

123. **Answer: C**

The PCAOB (specifically, AS Section 1220) identifies a number of differences relative to the AICPA's quality control standards, including those stated in the first, second, and last choices. However, the PCAOB requires the engagement quality review documentation to be retained along with (not separately from!) the related engagement documentation; and PCAOB auditing standards require such audit documentation to be retained for 7 years, not 10. Moreover, the AICPA's SQCS do not require that the engagement quality review documentation be retained along with the related audit documentation. Hence, C is correct.

124. **Answer: B**

The PCAOB (specifically, AS Section 1220) states: "An outside reviewer who is not already associated with a registered public accounting firm would become associated with the firm issuing the report if he or she . . . (1) receives compensation from the firm issuing the report for performing the review or (2) performs the review as agent for the firm issuing the report."

125. **Answer: D**

The PCAOB (specifically, AS Section 1220) requires the engagement quality reviewer to evaluate the significant judgments and conclusions of the engagement team by (1) holding discussions with the engagement partner and other members of the engagement team and (2) reviewing the engagement's audit documentation. The engagement quality reviewer is not expected to direct inquiries to client personnel or perform audit verification procedures to corroborate account balances, such as analytical procedures or tests of details. Hence, the last choice is the correct answer.

126. **Answer: D**

A CPA would not accept a client who was unwilling to make all financial records available. Access to all financial records would be a minimum requirement for the audit, and management is required to state in the management representation letter that all financial records and data have been made available to the auditors.

127. **Answer: A**

AU-C 210 (Terms of Engagement, paragraph 10) requires the following specific matters to be addressed in the engagement letter:

a. "The objective and scope of the audit of the financial statements.
b. The responsibilities of the auditor.
c. The responsibilities of management.
d. A statement that because of the inherent limitations of an audit, together with the inherent limitations of internal control, an unavoidable risk exists that some material misstatements may not be detected, even though the audit is properly planned and performed in accordance with GAAS.
e. Identification of the applicable financial reporting framework for the preparation of the financial statements.
f. Reference to the expected form and content of any reports to be issued by the auditor and a statement that circumstances may arise in which a report may differ from its expected form and content."

The example engagement letter provided in an appendix to that pronouncement identifies several specific responsibilities of management, including the following: "for the design, implementation, and maintenance of internal control relevant to the preparation and fair presentation of financial statements that are free from material misstatement, whether due to fraud or error."

128. **Answer: D**

AICPA standards addressing required communications between successor and predecessor auditors state that an auditor should not accept an engagement until the successor auditor's required communications with the predecessor auditor have been evaluated.

129. **Answer: B**

An engagement letter, which documents the agreed upon terms of the audit engagement, specifically addresses the respective responsibilities of management and the auditor, among other matters.

130. **Answer: A**

The engagement letter identifies the respective responsibilities of the entity and the auditor, and essentially constitutes the contract between the parties. It is customary for the engagement letter to address fee-related issues.

131. **Answer: B**

When it might be best (or even possible) to perform tests of control and substantive tests could be affected by the availability of underlying evidence.

132. **Answer: B**

ANY client-imposed scope limitation is a problem. When you add that problem to the greater risk arising from a new client, you have greatly increased the risk related to the new engagement. A new client, by definition, is a client that will require more time to study and understand in order to perform the audit. If the client is also telling the auditors that certain audit procedures will not be allowed, the risk of missing a material misstatement becomes very high.

133. **Answer: B**

The use of information technology in the accounting system greatly impacts the auditor's documentation of that system. For example, a highly automated system will result in very different documentation than a manual system.

134. **Answer: A**

In planning the overall audit strategy and designing the written audit plan, the auditor should consider materiality for the financial statements taken as a whole.

135. **Answer: A**

The auditor is required to obtain an understanding of the entity's environment, including internal control sufficient to plan the audit. Risk assessment is one of the five components of the internal control structure. Obtaining an understanding of the entity's risk assessment process would be part of obtaining an understanding of internal control.

136. **Answer: A**

The auditor is allowed to "pass" on aggregated errors that are not material. This analysis and conclusion must be documented in the audit documentation.

137. **Answer: B**

The auditor's preliminary judgment about materiality is a judgment about the amount of a misstatement in the financial statements under audit, which would be considered material (one that could influence the decision of a reasonable person relying on the financial statements). It is appropriate and likely, therefore, for the auditor to consider the entity's annualized interim financial statements in developing such a judgment.

138. **Answer: C**

Materiality refers to a cutoff amount for a misstatement over which the financial statements would be unfairly presented. In determining this amount, out of the choices given, the most likely source is the prior year financial statements. The statements would provide the auditor with the most information to use in setting materiality.

139. **Answer: B**

In order to issue an unqualified opinion, the auditor must be confident that no material misstatements exist in the financial statements. While misstatements may exist, in total they must be believed to be less than a material amount.

140. **Answer: D**

AICPA Professional Standards (specifically, *Materiality in Planning and Performing an Audit*) state, "If the auditor concludes that a lower materiality than that initially determined for the financial statements as a whole (and, if applicable, materiality level or levels for particular classes of transactions, account balances, or disclosures) is appropriate, the auditor should determine whether it is necessary to revise performance materiality and whether the nature, timing, and extent of the further audit procedures remain appropriate" (AU-C 320.13). Accordingly, if the auditor revises the planned materiality level at the financial statement level, the auditor should consider whether the planned materiality level(s) for particular classes of transactions, account balances, or disclosures should be revised as well.

141. **Answer: C**

Lowering the assessment of control risk would permit a somewhat higher level of detection risk. Taking a smaller sample size would be associated with a higher level of detection risk, which would be appropriate in view of the reduced control risk.

142. **Answer: B**

Inherent risk and control risk comprise the risk of material misstatement, which the auditor is obligated to assess. The auditor is responsible for designing the audit procedures to be responsive to the assessed risk of material misstatement, which exists independently of the audit itself.

143. **Answer: A**

Detection risk is inversely related to the assurance provided by substantive tests. The lower the detection risk, the more assurance needed from substantive testing.

144. **Answer: B**

The risk that an auditor will conclude, based on substantive tests, that a material error does not exist in an account balance when, in fact, such error does exist, is referred to as detection risk. Detection risk is a function of the effectiveness of an auditing procedure and its application by the auditor.

145. **Answer: D**

Inherent risk and control risk (also called environmental risks) are functions of the client and its environment, while detection risk is not. As a result, inherent risk and control risk can only be assessed by the auditor, while detection risk is controlled by the auditor.

146. **Answer: C**

Performing substantive tests at an interim date increases the risk that misstatements that exist at the balance sheet date will not be detected by the auditor. Evidence collected at an interim date is therefore less strong than evidence collected at year end. Increasing detection risk means that the auditor can obtain less or weaker evidence. As a result, the auditor may be able to push the timing of substantive tests from year end to an interim date.

147. **Answer: C**

An increase in the assessed level of control risk means that the risk of a material misstatement occurring and not being detected has increased. To offset that increased risk, the auditor should make decisions that decrease the level of detection risk. Increasing the emphasis on tests of details would decrease detection risk.

148. **Answer: C**

Inherent risk and control risk are environmental risks pertaining to the client. They are assessed by the auditor and exist independently of the financial statement audit. Detection risk is the only risk controllable by the auditor. It relates to the auditor's procedures and can be changed by the auditor.

149. **Answer: B**

When the level of tolerable misstatements decreases, the auditor will have to increase substantive testing to ensure that all material misstatements are detected. Performing the planned auditing procedures closer to the balance sheet date increases the effectiveness of substantive procedures and thus increases substantive testing.

150. **Answer: C**

A significant increase in net income would result in an increase, not a decrease, in retained earnings.

151. **Answer: B**

This ratio is total current liabilities divided by A/P. A decrease in this ratio (from 6:1 to 4:1) could be caused by an omission of current liabilities (other than A/P) resulting in the appearance that A/P is a larger proportion of total current liabilities than it should be.

152. **Answer: C**

Analytical procedures are defined as follows (AU-C 520.04): "Evaluations of financial information through analysis of plausible relationships among both financial and nonfinancial data. Analytical procedures also encompass such investigation, as is necessary, of identified fluctuations or relationships that are inconsistent with other relevant information or that differ from expected values by a significant amount." Accordingly, analytical procedures would be useful in identifying unusual year-end transactions.

153. **Answer: D**

Analytical procedures are a category of "substantive" audit procedures, and unexpected differences relative to the auditor's expectations may direct the auditor's attention to the possibility of a material misstatement.

154. **Answer: C**

In planning the audit engagement, an auditor likely would compare current-year balances with budgeted balances that would be useful in developing expectations.

155. **Answer: D**

Analytical procedures used in the overall review stage of an audit are intended to assist the auditor in assessing the conclusions reached and in evaluating the overall financial statement presentation.

156. **Answer: C**

Comparing the current and prior year's financial statements is a legitimate analytical procedure performed both in planning and as a final review.

157. **Answer: B**

Analytical procedures used in planning often use data aggregated at a high level.

158. **Answer: C**

Evaluating the characteristics of a population by means of applying statistical sampling techniques, specifically projecting a deviation or error rate, is likely to be performed as part of "test of controls," not an analytical procedure.

159. **Answer: A**

Although this is not a particularly good definition of "fraud," it is the best of the available answers. AICPA Professional Standards identify two types of fraud relevant to an audit: (1) fraudulent financial reporting, and (2) misappropriation of assets. The intent to deceive is an essential aspect of fraud. Fraud may be material or immaterial to the financial statements. In planning the audit engagement, the auditor focuses on detecting fraud that is material to the financial statements.

160. **Answer: D**

The risk of fraudulent financial reporting is heightened by the existence of an overly complex organizational structure involving unusual lines of authority. This type of structure would make it easier to override internal controls to materially misstate the financial statements.

161. **Answer: B**

An auditor would suspect material misstatements to be present if differences between reconciliations of control accounts and subsidiary records were not investigated.

Such differences should be investigated and corrected to ensure that control accounts and subsidiary records agree. Without this control, procedure material misstatements may exist in the form of differences between the control accounts and subsidiary records.

162. **Answer: D**

Professional Standards emphasize the importance of "professional skepticism" when considering fraud-related risks. Professional skepticism is described as "... an attitude that includes a questioning mind and a critical assessment of audit evidence."

163. **Answer: A**

Risk factors associated with opportunities to misappropriate assets include easily convertible assets, such as bearer bonds.

164. **Answer: D**

The substantial increase in sales in year 1 and substantial decrease in sales in year 2 is consistent with earnings management that might be associated with financial reporting fraud.

165. **Answer: C**

The auditor should routinely consider the reliability of audit evidence in assessing the risks of material misstatement whether due to fraud or error.

166. **Answer: D**

The determination of whether a misstatement is intentional (fraud) or unintentional (error) may be difficult, especially in subjective circumstances involving accounting estimates or the application of accounting principles.

167. **Answer: C**

Any fraud involving senior management, whether material or not, should be reported to those charged with governance.

168. **Answer: B**

Fraud that has been detected by the auditor and which is immaterial to the financial statements (and which does not involve senior management) should be reported to the appropriate level of management, at least one level above where the fraud is believed to have originated.

169. **Answer: D**

The existence of irregularities (fraud) is considered to be a severe problem in an audit due to potential ramifications for other areas of the audit. As a result, the auditor has a duty to disclose irregularities to the SEC when the client reports an auditor change, to a successor auditor when the successor makes appropriate inquiries, and to a government funding agency from which the client receives financial assistance.

170. **Answer: A**

In obtaining an understanding of the entity and its environment, the auditor should obtain an understanding of the entity's applicable legal and regulatory framework as well as how the entity complies with that framework.

171. **Answer: C**

The auditor may decide that withdrawal is necessary when the client fails to take the remedial action considered necessary. This failure may indicate a greater problem with the control environment and overall governance. As a result, it may affect the auditor's ability to rely on management representations as well as the relationship with the client going forward.

172. **Answer: B**

Doesn't this immediately raise questions?! Why would payments be made to government employees, especially unexplained payments? They sound like bribes.

173. Answer: B

Large checks payable to cash would be most likely to raise questions regarding possible illegal acts. Valid company disbursements are typically made by check and controlled through accounts payable. Cash payments are unusual and difficult to control. As a result, large checks payable to cash would present a red flag during the audit.

174. Answer: A

AICPA Professional Standards view a specialist as someone having specialized expertise outside of accounting and auditing whom the auditor uses, in effect, as a member of the audit team. Professional Standards include the interpretation of contracts, laws, and regulations as an example of such specialized expertise.

175. Answer: B

The auditor is required to gain an understanding of the relationship and assess the risk that the actuary's objectivity might be impaired. Impairment might occur when the client has the ability to directly, or indirectly, control or significantly influence the actuary.

176. Answer: A

When using a specialist, in general, the auditor is obligated to obtain an understanding of the work to be performed by the specialist, including the nature, objectives, and scope of the specialist's work.

177. Answer: C

AICPA Professional Standards indicate that reference to the work of a specialist may be made in the auditor's report if the auditor believes such reference will facilitate an understanding of the reason for a modified opinion.

178. Answer: D

The auditor should obtain an understanding of the specialist's field of expertise sufficient to enable determination of the nature, objectives, and scope of the specialist's work and evaluation of the adequacy of that work. This includes obtaining an understanding of the significant assumptions and methods used by the specialist.

179. Answer: B

During the planning, the auditor will communicate that the audit does not relieve management of its responsibilities for the financial statements.

180. Answer: B

All uncorrected misstatements must be communicated to the audit committee (or those charged with governance), unless they are deemed to be trivial.

181. Answer: B

The maximum dollar amount of misstatements, that could exist without causing the financial statements to be materially misstated, is an auditor judgment. The auditor's determination of materiality levels is generally NOT discussed with the audit committee.

182. Answer: B

The auditor is required to communicate with an entity's audit committee (or those charged with governance) about such matters as significant accounting policies, management judgments and accounting estimates, significant audit adjustments, disagreements with management, consultation with other accountants, and difficulties encountered in performing the audit. Management changes in the application of significant accounting policies are included in this list of matters to be communicated.

183. Answer: C

The auditor is required to communicate disagreements with management to those charged with governance that arose during the audit about matters that are individually or in the aggregate significant to the financial statements or the auditor's report.

184. Answer: C

The auditor is required to communicate with the audit committee about changes in the application of significant accounting principles.

185. Answer: A

An audit committee is a subset of the board of directors that is comprised of board members who are independent of the entity's management.

186. **Answer: A**

     PCAOB AS Section 1301identifies the following four objectives: (1) communicate to the audit committee the auditor's responsibilities and establish an understanding of the terms of the engagement; (2) obtain information from the audit committee relevant to the audit; (3) communicate to the audit committee information about the strategy and timing of the audit; and (4) provide the audit committee with timely observations about significant audit matters. These objectives do not include enhancing communications between the audit committee and the entity's internal audit function.

187. **Answer: C**

     Although the auditor would discuss with the audit committee the qualitative aspects of the entity's significant accounting policies (and any indications of management bias), those matters would be discussed at the end of the audit.

188. **Answer: D**

     Unless otherwise specified, the communication may be written or oral. (For example, an engagement letter obviously must be in writing.) The PCAOB requires that the communication be timely and prior to the issuance of the auditor's report.

189. **Answer: B**

     Obtaining an understanding of an entity's internal controls over financial reporting involves evaluating the design of relevant controls and determining whether they have been implemented (sometimes referred to as "placed into operation").

190. **Answer: D**

     The auditor is primarily interested in whether an entity's internal controls affect the financial statement assertions. Specifically, the auditor is interested in the policies and procedures that pertain to an entity's ability to record, process, summarize, and report financial data consistent with the assertions embodied in the financial statements.

191. **Answer: D**

     If the auditor has concluded that an account is immaterial and that inherent risk is low, the auditor might decide to skip the procedures used to obtain an understanding of the related internal controls because the risk of a material misstatement occurring is low.

     This is really a rather tricky question because GAAS require the auditor to obtain an understanding of the internal control structure sufficient to plan the audit. In the case of immateriality combined with low inherent risk, the auditor does not need to understand the internal controls specifically related to the account in order to plan the audit.

192. **Answer: B**

     A decision table presents in tabular form the conditions and alternative actions related to making a particular decision. It emphasizes logical relationships (decision rules) among the conditions and actions.

193. **Answer: C**

     The use of budgets and forecasts to compare planned and actual results will enable management to supervise more effectively than the other controls listed. It provides a means for management to establish expectations, to compare them to actual results, and then to follow up in areas where significant differences appeared. Monitoring compliance with regulatory requirements, limiting access to assets, and providing adequate support are important to the successful operation of the business but they do not necessarily help management to supervise more effectively.

194. **Answer: C**

     The auditor is always required to obtain a sufficient understanding of the internal control system in order to plan the audit. This understanding must be documented, regardless of the level at which control risk is to be assessed. Control activities and control environment factors are both components of the internal control system. As a result, they would both be documented.

195. **Answer: C**

     The auditor assesses control risk for the assertions present in the financial statements. Such assertions may be found in the account balance, transaction class, or disclosure components. Based on the understanding of internal control and the control risk assessments, the auditor determines the nature, timing, and extent of the auditing procedures to be performed.

196. Answer: A

After obtaining an understanding of internal control and assessing control risk, an auditor will perform tests of controls, if it is believed that such performance will result in a reduction in planned substantive tests. If the performance of tests of controls would not result in a reduction in substantive testing, completing tests of controls would be inefficient and therefore should not be performed.

197. Answer: B

The auditor would decide that an audit could not be conducted if management integrity were questioned. Management integrity is such a critical component of an effective internal control environment that the suspected lack thereof would be cause for the auditor to withdraw from the engagement.

198. Answer: A

Understanding internal control and assessing control risk are steps that may be performed concurrently in an audit. The evidence collected to achieve one objective may also be used for the other objective. For example, inquiries and information gathered about management's use of budgets in order to understand the control environment may also be used as a test of control over the effectiveness and operation of the budgeting control.

199. Answer: D

In order to assess control risk below maximum, the auditor must collect evidence to support the reduction. Collecting such evidence involves identifying specific internal controls relevant to specific assertions and then performing tests of controls to evaluate the effectiveness of the controls.

200. Answer: D

If the auditor desires to further reduce the assessed level of control risk, he/she must first consider whether additional evidence will be available to support such a reduction. The auditor must also consider whether it would be efficient (cost-effective) to collect such evidence.

201. Answer: C

The auditor is always required to obtain a sufficient understanding of the internal control system in order to plan the audit. This understanding must be documented, regardless of the level at which control risk is to be assessed. Control activities and control environment factors are both components of the internal control system. As a result, they would both be documented.

202. Answer: A

When a deviation from a prescribed control procedure occurs, the auditor should evaluate the significance of the potential effects associated with the deficiency. It would be appropriate to make inquiry of management and other client personnel in evaluating the potential effect of such a control deficiency.

203. Answer: C

COSO's Internal Control Integrated Framework identifies five components of an internal control system: (1) control environment; (2) risk assessment; (3) control activities; (4) information and communication system; and (5) monitoring. Accordingly, inherent risk is not one of those components.

204. Answer: D

Closer management oversight directed specifically at such incompatible activities would be an effective approach in mitigating the risks involved.

205. Answer: D

Internal control can provide only reasonable assurance as a limiting factor is the cost/benefit ratio. The cost of an entity's internal control should not exceed the benefits derived therefrom.

206. Answer: A

In obtaining an understanding of an entity's internal controls that are relevant to audit planning, an auditor is required to obtain knowledge about the design of relevant internal controls pertaining to financial reporting in each of the five internal control components. Note that only those internal controls which impact the financial statements are to be considered. It is not necessary to understand and evaluate all of an entity's internal controls.

207. **Answer: D**

The auditor would conclude that a financial audit could not be performed if he/she determined that a substantial risk of intentional misapplication of accounting principles existed.

The key word is "intentional" as the risk of management override is an inherent limitation of any internal control system. Management can override the system to make material misstatements in the financial statements and the auditors may not be able to detect such entries.

If management is believed to be intentionally misapplying accounting principles, the financial statements are likely to contain material misstatements that may be extremely difficult, if not impossible, to detect. Thus, the auditors would withdraw from the engagement.

208. **Answer: C**

When evidence is available only in electronic form, the auditor may find that generalized audit software is the best and most efficient means of extracting evidence from client databases. Generalized audit software consists of programs that enable an auditor to perform tests on client computer files and databases.

209. **Answer: B**

Inquiry and observation may be useful in evaluating the effectiveness of internal controls, including those that are undocumented.

210. **Answer: A**

Control risk is assessed in terms of the financial statement assertions. The auditor may assess control risk at maximum because the controls do not pertain to the assertions, or are ineffective, or because testing such controls would not result in a reduction in substantive testing (would be inefficient).

211. **Answer: D**

The objective of tests of details of transactions performed as tests of controls is to evaluate whether internal controls operated effectively. A test of details of transactions performed as a test of control will enable the auditor to detect a control failure.

212. **Answer: C**

A significant deficiency is a control deficiency in the design or operation of internal control that can adversely affect the financial statements.

If those responsible for accounting decisions appear to lack objectivity, the resultant accounting decisions may result in material misstatements of the financial statements.

For example, revenue recognition decisions might be made to increase current period net income (and managerial bonuses).

213. **Answer: C**

A significant deficiency is a control deficiency in the design or operation of internal control that can adversely affect the entity's ability to initiate, record, process, and report financial data in the financial statements.

Factors to be considered in evaluating deficiencies include the entity's size, its complexity, and the nature and diversity of its business activities.

214. **Answer: C**

Significant deficiencies should be reported to the audit committee because they are significant deficiencies in the design or operation of internal control that could adversely affect the entity's financial reporting process.

215. **Answer: A**

The definition of a significant deficiency states that a significant deficiency is less severe than a material weakness.

216. **Answer: C**

AICPA Professional Standards (specifically, *Communicating Internal Control Related Matters Identified in an Audit*) requires the auditor to communicate to those charged with governance any "significant deficiencies" in internal control identified by the auditor. The auditor is not required to communicate all control deficiencies identified.

217. **Answer: D**

The auditor would appropriately discuss the planned scope and timing of the audit at a fairly general (strategic) level with those charged with governance.

218. **Answer: A**

Internal auditing standards developed by The Institute of Internal Auditors address independence and objectivity and thus might be considered by an independent CPA in assessing the objectivity of internal auditors.

In addition, the independent CPA would consider whether the internal auditor reports to an officer of sufficient status, whether the internal auditor has direct access to the board of directors and the audit committee, whether internal audit employment decisions are overseen by the board of directors and/or the audit committee, and whether policies exist to prohibit the audit of areas in which conflicts of interest exist.

219. **Answer: B**

AICPA Professional Standards indicate that the auditor should assess the competence and objectivity of the internal audit function if the internal auditors' work is considered relevant to planning the audit. The independent auditor would consider the quality of the internal auditor's work products, including documentation, among other matters, in evaluating the internal auditor's competence.

220. **Answer: A**

When assessing the internal auditor's objectivity, the auditor should consider (1) the organizational status of the internal audit function; and (2) the policies affecting the internal auditor's objectivity about areas audited. The latter includes policies prohibiting the internal auditor from auditing areas where recently assigned.

221. **Answer: B**

In evaluating the internal auditors' competence, the auditor should obtain (or update) information about: educational level and professional experience; professional certification and continuing education; policies related to assignment of internal auditors; policies related to supervision and review; quality of work products; and performance evaluations.

222. **Answer: D**

The internal auditors' work may affect the independent auditors' work in all three areas. When such work is expected to affect the audit, the independent auditor must evaluate its quality and effectiveness in order to determine the extent to which such work may be relied upon. Note that even when the internal auditors' work is to be used, the independent auditor is still responsible for ensuring that sufficient, competent evidential matter is obtained to support the opinion.

223. **Answer: D**

The auditor may use internal auditors to provide direct assistance in performing tests of controls and/or substantive procedures, but the auditor is still responsible for all conclusions reached and should appropriately supervise, review, evaluate, and test the internal auditors' work.

224. **Answer: A**

If the auditor is concerned that invoices and vouchers are being paid and destroyed, the most appropriate population for testing is cash disbursements.

The auditor would select a sample of inventory disbursements and trace to the vendor invoice, approved voucher, and receiving report.

225. **Answer: D**

Segregation of duties involves the separation of the responsibilities of authorizing transactions, recording transactions, and maintaining custody of assets. It is intended to reduce the opportunities for any person to be in a position to both perpetrate and conceal errors or irregularities in the normal course of his/her duties.

226. **Answer: C**

An entity's invoices should be identified by unique invoice numbers. If multiple invoices have the same invoice number, there may be an underlying intention to deceive or conceal certain transactions, which is consistent with possible fraud.

227. **Answer: B**

In testing the completeness assertion (regarding omissions) related to sales and receivables, the auditor starts with a source document and agrees the item to the accounting records. Starting with a shipping document and tracing it to the sales journal (i.e., to a sales invoice recorded in the sales journal) would be an appropriate test for unrecorded sales and receivables.

228. **Answer: D**

Authorization of write-offs should be made by a department independent of recording or authorization duties pertaining to accounts receivable. The accounts receivable department maintains the accounts receivable records; the credit department approves credit for customers. Neither, therefore, is a good candidate for authorizing write-offs. Assigning the accounts payable department doesn't make sense. This leaves the treasurer as the best candidate for authorization of write-offs.

229. **Answer: C**

Effective internal controls include adequate segregation of duties. The failure to separate authorization of credit memos from cash handling is a segregation of duties failure in the revenue cycle.

230. **Answer: B**

An auditor would suspect material misstatements to be present if differences between reconciliations of control accounts and subsidiary records were not investigated. Such differences should be investigated and corrected to ensure that control accounts and subsidiary records agree. Without this control procedure material misstatements may exist in the form of differences between the control accounts and subsidiary records.

231. **Answer: C**

The greatest risk for checks received in the mail is the risk of such checks being lost or misappropriated. Sound internal control, therefore, dictates the preparation of a listing of checks received as soon as possible.

232. **Answer: A**

Establishing a bank lockbox system would provide the best control over customer receipts because it would prevent the employees from having access to the receipts.

233. **Answer: B**

Substantive tests of sales transactions would be limited when control risk is assessed as low for existence/occurrence and evidence has been gathered supporting cash receipts and accounts receivable. Consider the accounts which are impacted by sales transactions, DR Cash or Accounts Receivable and CR Sales. The combination of low control risk in this area plus evidence supporting cash receipts and accounts receivable provides the auditor with assurance that sales transactions have actually occurred.

234. **Answer: C**

Allowing the bookkeeper to have access to the accounting records and to the signature plates, which effectively enables the bookkeeper to initiate unauthorized transactions, while also having responsibility for preparing the monthly bank reconciliations is an improper segregation of duties.

235. **Answer: C**

An effective procedure to prevent duplicate payments is to cancel the documentation supporting the payment request at the time payment is made. For example, by stamping the documents as "paid."

236. **Answer: B**

This question pertains to segregation of duties. An employee responsible for matching vendor invoices with receiving reports is performing a step in the authorization process which will result in invoices being approved for payment. The same employee should not have responsibility for posting the accounts payable records, reconciling the accounts payable ledger, or canceling invoices after payment, as each would provide an opportunity for embezzlement or misappropriation to occur. It would be acceptable for the employee to recompute the calculations on vendors' invoices, which would be an additional step in the same authorization process.

237. **Answer: D**

To provide for adequate segregation of duties, the person who signs checks should also be responsible for mailing the checks. Having the signer mail the checks eliminates the opportunity for the check preparer or others with conflicting duties to modify and/or divert the checks before mailing.

238. **Answer: D**

The approval of employee hours by the departmental supervisor is a control which helps to ensure that only hours worked are paid. This reduces the chance that employees will submit hours that were not actually worked or were unauthorized.

239. **Answer: D**

The approval of time cards by supervisors helps to ensure that payment is made only for work performed. The supervisor's approval indicates that the employee has indeed worked the hours indicated on the time card. The approved hours per the time card will then be paid. Thus, payment is made only for work performed.

240. **Answer: B**

Management's objectives in establishing and maintaining an internal control structure are to ensure that:

1) transactions are executed in accordance with management's general or specific authorization;

2) transactions are recorded as necessary to permit preparation of the financial statements in accordance with GAAP and to maintain accountability for assets;

3) access to assets is permitted only in accordance with management's authorization; and

4) the recorded accountability for assets is compared with the existing assets at reasonable intervals and differences are investigated and resolved. Ensuring that custody of work in process and of finished goods is properly maintained is an example of the third objective.

241. **Answer: D**

An internal control questionnaire for notes payable would ask about controls over direct borrowings on notes payable. The concern would be whether it was possible for borrowings to occur without proper authorization.

242. **Answer: C**

The most effective control to prevent direct labor hours from being charged to manufacturing overhead is the use of time tickets to record actual labor worked on production orders. The time tickets, in turn, are posted to the work-in-process records,

providing greater assurance that direct labor is being properly charged.

243. **Answer: A**

The concealment of fraud pertaining to marketable securities is best controlled through controlling access and providing for adequate segregation of duties. Use of a trust company aids in both respects. Access to the marketable securities is controlled by the trust company, an independent entity, and the duties of authorization and recording are automatically separated from the duty of custody. By limiting the trust company's direct contact with employees responsible for recordkeeping, the potential for fraud is further lessened as segregation of duties is increased.

244. **Answer: C**

The assessment of control risk at a low level requires that the auditor provide the basis for reducing the assessment. The basis is provided by performing tests of controls and documenting the results which support a lowered control risk assessment. In turn, the low control risk assessment enables the auditor to reduce the amount of substantive testing in that area, thus limiting the testing of current year property and equipment transactions.

245. **Answer: C**

The auditor would seek to obtain the additional evidence needed to support the valuation of inventory.

246. **Answer: C**

This ratio is called "inventory turnover," which is a traditional ratio that is useful in evaluating whether inventory might be slow-moving. In that event, inventory might need to be written down to better reflect the estimated future benefits. This might be appropriately considered in the partner's review.

247. **Answer: D**

Determination of the timing of inventory observation procedures to be performed would be most likely to be agreed upon with the client before implementation, because the auditor would need to be informed as to the timing of, and procedures related to, the physical inventory-taking by the client.

248. **Answer: A**

As the risk of material misstatement increases, the auditor should decrease detection risk accordingly. The auditor may lower detection risk by increasing the extent of substantive procedures (e.g., by increasing sample sizes).

249. **Answer: A**

Analytical procedures are defined as "evaluations of financial information through analysis of plausible relationships among both financial and nonfinancial data." That definition encompasses evaluating the current-year balances by comparing them to prior-year balances for reasonableness.

250. **Answer: C**

Follow-up on errors reported by customers provides evidence that the customers exist and that the receivables are valid; i.e., that the client has the rights to the assets. The auditor's test of controls thus provides evidence to support the assertion of rights and obligations. It does not address presentation and disclosure.

251. **Answer: C**

There are 4 assertions applicable to account balances at the period end: (1) existence; (2) completeness; (3) rights or obligations; and (4) valuation and allocation.

252. **Answer: C**

Greater reliability (and thus, persuasiveness) is achieved from evidence obtained from sources outside the entity, even when that evidence is obtained from the client.

253. **Answer: D**

Professional judgement is required to determine when sufficient appropriate audit evidence has been obtained as a reasonable basis for the auditor's conclusions.

254. **Answer: A**

Determining whether all sales have, in fact, been recorded addresses the risk of omission, which involves the completeness assertion.

255. **Answer: D**

During the overall review stage, the auditor assesses the conclusions reached and the evaluation of the overall financial statement presentation. As part of that evaluation, he/she would consider whether the results of the audit procedures performed affect the risk of material misstatement due to fraud. The overall review would include considering the adequacy of the evidence gathered in response to unusual or unexpected balances and whether such balances reflected a misstatement due to fraud.

256. **Answer: D**

The auditor would consider the difficulty in controlling the incremental audit risk, i.e., the risk that material misstatements will not be detected due to the early testing at interim. This difficulty would be impacted by the effectiveness of internal controls, the presence of rapidly changing business conditions or circumstances, and the availability of relevant information.

257. **Answer: C**

This is a test of controls. The auditor is verifying that segregation of duties exists and is operating effectively.

258. **Answer: C**

Audit procedures should be responsive to the auditor's assessment of the risks of material misstatement. The specific procedures that are appropriate in the circumstances is a matter of professional judgment.

259. **Answer: D**

The auditor should consider whether the assessments of the risks of material misstatement at the relevant assertion level in engagement planning are appropriate in light of the auditor's substantive procedures.

260. **Answer: D**

AICPA Professional Standards (specifically, AU-C 500, *Audit Evidence*) identifies seven types of audit procedures: (1) inspection; (2) observation; (3) external confirmation; (4) recalculation; (5) reperformance; (6) inquiry; and (7) analytical procedures. The AICPA describes examining accounting records as "inspection."

261. **Answer: C**

"Cutoff" was not identified as one of five financial assertions discussed by the PCAOB. The AICPA's risk assessment standards identify 13 assertions across three categories of assertions. And one of those is "cutoff," which is included among the assertions associated with "transactions or events during the period."

262. **Answer: A**

The auditor should incorporate a degree of unpredictability in planning audit procedures, but this is considered an "overall response" to the risks of material misstatement, not a "risk assessment procedure."

263. **Answer: B**

The word "could" does not indicate a professional requirement. Instead, it indicates an audit consideration that is based on the auditor's professional judgment.

264. **Answer: A**

In determining whether identified (uncorrected) misstatements are material in the aggregate, the auditor should take into consideration the effects of relevant misstatements identified in a prior period, even if they were deemed immaterial in the prior period.

265. **Answer: B**

The auditor should request management to correct (non-trivial) identified factual misstatements.

266. **Answer: C**

The auditor should not divulge to management the specific levels of materiality used or the materiality levels allocated to individual elements of the financial statements. So obtaining such agreement would not be appropriate.

267. **Answer: A**

The definition of judgmental misstatements includes unreasonable accounting estimates (as well as the selection of inappropriate accounting policies).

268. **Answer: A**

AICPA Professional Standards describe the term "judgmental misstatement" as follows: "differences in estimates, such as a difference in a fair value estimate" (AU-C 450. A11).

269. **Answer: D**

After the documentation completion date, the auditor is prohibited from deleting any of the existing audit documentation.

270. **Answer: A**

Among other matters, auditors should document all significant audit findings or issues, which include any matters that could result in modification of the auditor's report.

271. **Answer: C**

The working trial balance would NOT appear in the permanent file. It is normally included in the current year audit documentation.

272. **Answer: A**

Notes receivable and interest income would most likely be analyzed on the same working paper as they are directly related to each other. Interest income is earned on notes receivable and is a function of the interest rate and the principal balances on the notes.

273. **Answer: A**

Audit documentation serves mainly to provide the principal support for the opinion rendered in the auditor's report. It also aids the auditor in the conduct and supervision of the audit.

274. **Answer: C**

PCAOB auditing standards specify a 7-year retention period for audit documentation.

275. **Answer: B**

PCAOB auditing standards specify a documentation completion date of no more than 45 days following the report release date.

276. **Answer: B**

PCAOB Auditing Standards state that additional documentation can be added after the documentation completion date (which requires further documentation of the reasons why, etc.), but nothing can be deleted after that date.

277. **Answer: C**

AICPA Professional Standards indicate that using blank confirmation requests may provide a greater degree of assurance about the information confirmed because of the need to fill in the amount. However, blank forms might also result in lower response rates because additional effort is required of the recipients. When lower response rates occur, the auditor may have to perform more alternative procedures making the confirmation effort less efficient.

278. **Answer: D**

The auditor would be more likely to confirm certain relevant contract terms as the risk of material misstatement increases. In this case, the risk of material misstatement is said to be "high," which is consistent with the need to perform additional procedures to address revenue-recognition issues.

279. **Answer: A**

When negative confirmations are used, the respondent is asked to return the request only if there is a problem or error in the balance. Thus, it is assumed that the balances are correct unless the confirmation is returned. Unreturned negative confirmation requests, therefore, are considered to be evidence. This evidence is implied, it is not explicit.

280. **Answer: B**

To ensure that a fax is valid, the auditor would need to perform other procedures that would aid in verifying the authenticity of the fax. Telephoning the sender would provide additional evidence that the fax was authentic.

281. **Answer: A**

Using the blank form of confirmation of accounts receivable provides greater assurance that the recipient of the confirmation has verified that the information is correct. It is more likely to be used when the auditor is concerned that recipients will not devote proper attention to the confirmations.

282. **Answer: D**

If the auditor is concerned about identifying all material accounting estimates, the auditor is seeking to discover unrecorded estimates. The auditor is most likely to review the lawyer's letter for information about litigation. Litigation losses is an area that commonly requires estimates and one in which estimates could be material to the financial statements.

It is also an area that falls outside of the normal financial reporting process and, thus, is more likely to be missed.

283. **Answer: A**

This question focuses on something that would be a "concern" to the auditor about an accounting estimate. To the extent that the estimate is potentially biased (e.g., perhaps management has a lot of latitude in determining the resulting estimate), the auditor would be concerned about the reasonableness of that estimate.

284. **Answer: A**

AICPA Professional Standards indicate that the auditor is responsible for evaluating the reasonableness of accounting estimates made by management in the context of the applicable financial reporting framework.

285. **Answer: D**

Obtaining a current appraisal of the collateral would be directly relevant to establishing the current value of that collateral.

286. **Answer: B**

When an active trading market for debt securities has been introduced in the current year, the fair value of the debt securities would be based on that active trading market. However, the prior year's financial statements presented for comparative purposes would still be based on the model selected by management. Hence, consistency in the model's application would not be maintained.

287. **Answer: A**

The auditor will consider whether or not the nature of significant assumptions used in fair value measurements, the degree of subjectivity involved in the development of the assumptions, and the relative materiality of the items being measured at fair value need to be communicated to those charged with governance.

288. Answer: C

This is not an accurate characterization of the auditor's responsibilities. The decision to engage a specialist is a matter of professional judgment. The auditor may have the necessary skill and knowledge to audit fair values or may decide to use a specialist.

289. Answer: B

The decision to engage a specialist is an auditor judgment, not a management decision.

290. Answer: D

A taxing authority could impose an assessment on an entity related to tax matters. The auditor might then identify the existence of such an assessment by reviewing correspondence between the entity and the taxing authority.

291. Answer: C

The auditor will often seek to obtain an attorney's letter, as that provides some of the primary evidence supporting litigation, claims, and assessments. Note that the question indicates that the auditor is corroborating information. The auditor first obtains the information from the client. That information is then corroborated by the information obtained from the attorney.

292. Answer: B

This comment is extremely vague and clarification would be required. What exactly would this mean? In litigation, settlements are always less than the damages claimed! This is part of the negotiation process.

293. Answer: C

Issues that are significant to the entity (for example, litigation issues that result in contingent liabilities) normally rise to the level of discussion by those charged with governance. The auditor routinely reads the minutes of these meetings to identify issues that have financial reporting implications, including issues related to contingent liabilities.

294. Answer: A

A management representation letter routinely requires management to take responsibility for the design, implementation, and maintenance of programs and controls to detect fraud.

295. Answer: C

The purpose of the "summary of unadjusted differences" is to determine whether identified differences between the accounting records and the audit evidence that are not individually material might be material in the aggregate. These items represent differences already identified and are not applicable to supporting management's responses to the auditor's inquiries.

296. Answer: A

This is a required item in the management representation letter. Management must acknowledge its responsibility for the design and implementation of programs and controls to prevent and detect fraud.

297. Answer: B

A management representation letter routinely includes a statement pointing out that senior management has no knowledge of any fraud or suspected fraud involving management, which includes the CFO.

298. Answer: B

The management representation letter should address all periods covered by the auditor's report. Key's management representation letter, therefore, should cover the two periods being audited up through the date of the report, i.e., from January 1, 2005, through May 1, 2007. This requirement exists even if management was not present during all periods covered by the auditor's report.

299. Answer: B

Reviewing conflict-of-interest statements signed by management would provide the auditor with information about potential relationships with related parties that might warrant additional disclosure in the financial statements.

300. Answer: D

GAAP focuses on providing full disclosure of related party issues, so the auditor places primary emphasis on evaluating the adequacy of disclosure of such transactions.

301. **Answer: C**

When auditing related party transactions, the auditor is primarily concerned with the adequacy of disclosure.

302. **Answer: C**

Reviewing confirmation of loans receivable and payable for indications of guarantees is one of the auditing procedures that will assist the auditor in identifying related party transactions.

303. **Answer: C**

The PCAOB requires the auditor to obtain an understanding of the company's process for the following: (1) identifying related parties and transactions with related parties; (2) authorizing and approving transactions with related parties; and (3) accounting for and disclosing relationships and transactions with related parties in the financial statements. There is no reason to expect that related-party transactions will have terms substantially equivalent to those associated with transactions with unrelated parties.

304. **Answer: B**

The PCAOB does not require the auditor to communicate with the audit committee about management's justification for engaging in transactions with a related party instead of with an unrelated party. Indeed, the company should have an appropriate process established to authorize and approve transactions with related parties, which presumably informs the audit committee as necessary.

305. **Answer: C**

PCAOB auditing standards (specifically, AS Section 2410) state that the auditor should consider a qualified or adverse opinion under such circumstances.

306. **Answer: A**

Correct!) GAAP requires that material changes in debt (or capital) structure during the subsequent events period be disclosed in the financial statements. Such changes would not require adjustment.

307. **Answer: D**

When such facts are discovered after the report release date, the auditor has an obligation to discuss the matter with management and determine whether the financial statements require revision. If so, then management's willingness to issue revised financial statements to known users of the entity's financial statements is a primary concern to the auditor.

308. **Answer: C**

Events that did not exist at year end but arose after year end require disclosure.

309. **Answer: A**

The auditor may not have to perform the omitted confirmation procedures if alternative (redundant) procedures compensate for the omission and limit audit risk to an acceptably low level.

310. **Answer: C**

The auditor should immediately gather sufficient appropriate audit evidence with respect to the receivables in question in order to determine whether the financial statements are fairly stated and whether the previously expressed opinion is appropriate.

311. **Answer: D**

Neither of those phrases is appropriate. "Except for..." is language used to identify a qualification for a departure from the applicable accounting framework. Since the entity's financial statements adequately disclose the uncertainties surrounding the going concern issue, a qualification is not appropriate. The phrase "possible discontinuance of the entity's operations" is not consistent with language suggested in AICPA Professional Standards, which, instead, offer the phrase "substantial doubt about the entity's ability to continue as a going concern."

312. **Answer: D**

The normal effect of violating the terms of debt agreements (including debt covenants) is to render the associated debt immediately due, which may cause significant financial stress on the entity and cause the auditor to have substantial doubt about the entity's ability to continue as a going concern.

313. **Answer: C**

In evaluating management's plans to deal with the adverse effects of conditions and events, the auditor may appropriately consider the feasibility of management's plans for disposal of certain assets.

314. **Answer: D**

When the auditor has substantial doubt about an entity's ability to continue as a going concern, the auditor's primary focus will be on the financial statement effects, especially the adequacy of disclosure of the matters raising the going concern issue.

315. **Answer: D**

Cooper would consider Zero's plans to postpone expenditures for research and development projects, as such plans would reduce the cash requirements for future periods and provide the company with additional flexibility, if needed.

316. **Answer: A**

GAAS indicate that external confirmations are frequently used to verify account balances. In doing so, they provide stronger evidence for the existence assertion than for the other assertions identified.

317. **Answer: C**

"Classification" is included among the five assertions associated with "classes of transactions and events for the period under audit," as identified by GAAS.

318. **Answer: B**

Tests of control are not a "substantive" procedure.

319. **Answer: A**

A cut-off bank statement is a regular bank statement that is prepared by the bank for a shorter period than normal. It is sent directly to (or picked up by) the auditors.

The cut-off bank statement is used by the auditors to verify the components of the client's bank reconciliation. The auditor would trace the prior year checks clearing in the cut-off statement to the outstanding check list in the bank reconciliation as a means of verifying the completeness and accuracy of the outstanding check list.

320. **Answer: C**

Check kiting occurs when cash is fraudulently created through the transfer of money between banks. Insufficient funds checks are written and deposited among a series of banks and the float is used to "create" cash.

Kiting would be evidenced by a low average balance compared to a high level of deposits because, although deposits are being made, checks are immediately written to remove the funds, resulting in a low average balance.

321. **Answer: A**

Much of the work done to audit the statement of cash flows consists of agreeing amounts included in the statement of cash flows to amounts reported in the other financial statements. This would include, for example, agreeing depreciation expense to the amount reported in the income statement.

322. **Answer: A**

In planning the sample, the auditor must determine how many and how much, i.e., how many cash receipts and what dollar cut-off. Both are affected by materiality levels.

323. **Answer: C**

The interview of the controller is "inquiry"; the review of the bank reconciliation for evidence that the control procedure of interest was performed (and initialed as performed) is "inspection of records."

324. **Answer: B**

When no response has been received for a positive confirmation, the first follow-up procedure would be to send a second request.

325. **Answer: B**

A difficulty commonly encountered by recipients of a confirmation request is the inability to determine what has been included in a given accounts receivable balance. Providing a list of the items or invoices making up the balance will facilitate the customer's reconciliation efforts and make it easier to respond to a confirmation request.

326. **Answer: B**

There is a presumption that the auditor will confirm selected receivables when they are material.

327. **Answer: D**

AICPA Professional Standards discuss responses to the auditor's assessment of the risks of material misstatement at two levels: (1) overall response and (2) response at the relevant assertion level. At the overall level, the auditor might assign more experienced staff to the engagement in response to a higher risk of material misstatement.

328. **Answer: C**

A positive confirmation test requests a response whether the individual customer agrees or disagrees with the stated balance. A nonresponse indicates a situation that should be followed up by the auditor.

329. **Answer: B**

Performing a trend analysis of quarterly sales is an analytical procedure that would be relevant to identifying unusual sales activities.

330. **Answer: B**

An entity's physical count of inventory establishes that the inventory exists.

331. **Answer: D**

Validity pertains to existence—that inventory is real and exists. Agreeing items in the inventory listing (which might be thought of as the subsidiary ledger for the adjusted general ledger balance for inventory) to the underlying inventory tags and the auditor's recorded count sheets provides support that the inventory in the listing actually exists. The direction of the test is critical to determining whether existence or completeness is most involved.

332. **Answer: D**

The completeness assertion pertains to transactions that have not been recorded or are missing. Performing cut-off procedures for shipping and receiving enables the auditor to detect late transactions that may not have been recorded in the proper period and may be missing from the current (audit) year.

333. **Answer: A**

The direction of the test is critical to the resulting inference. This test involves tracing from a type of source document (the count "tags") to the accounting records (since the computerized listing of inventory items is, in effect, the subsidiary ledger that supports the inventory-adjusted general ledger balance). Hence, this test addresses the "completeness" assertion by dealing with the risk of omission.

334. **Answer: C**

A "dual-purpose" test involves gathering evidence in part to evaluate the effectiveness of internal control and in part to evaluate the fairness of the financial statements. "Tests of controls" address the internal control part of the dual-purpose test; and the inspection of underlying accounting documents constitutes a test of details, which addresses the substantive part of the dual-purpose test.

335. **Answer: B**

Publicly traded stock is commonly held by a custodian on behalf of the investor. It would be most efficient and effective to confirm the number of shares owned with the independent custodian.

336. **Answer: C**

To establish the "reasonableness" of dividends on investments in public companies, the auditor might find relevant corroborating information using the Internet, such as visiting the SEC's website for information about dividends pertaining to investee companies.

337. **Answer: C**

To verify the year-end fair value of marketable securities, trace to an independent outside source, such as the *Wall Street Journal* or other appropriate quotation.

338. **Answer: B**

The rights and obligations assertion deals with whether the entity has the rights to or is obligated for the assets and liabilities in the financial statements. Confirming with an outside agent that the agent is holding securities in the client's name would address the existence of, and the client's rights to, such assets.

339. **Answer: D**

Debits that appear in repairs and maintenance expense have not been capitalized. A careful analysis of those charges will enable the auditor to identify major repairs and other expenditures that should have been capitalized.

340. **Answer: C**

The auditor analyzes repair and maintenance expense to identify amounts expensed that should have been capitalized.

341. **Answer: D**

The retirement of plant assets would result in a debit to accumulated depreciation, along with a credit to the plant assets account for the acquisition cost.

342. **Answer: A**

Agreeing the recorded additions of fixed assets to the underlying invoices and verifying that the assets have actually been placed in service (perhaps by inspecting the assets) establishes that the recorded assets are properly recorded, which is the essence of the existence assertion.

343. **Answer: B**

Significant debits to the accumulated depreciation accounts occur when plant assets are retired. The other choices are incorrect, as the impact on accumulated depreciation would be a credit or represent no effect.

344. **Answer: A**

The procedures used to identify unrecorded trade accounts payable are included in the basket of procedures performed as the search for unrecorded liabilities. Reviewing subsequent cash disbursements enables the auditor to detect items purchased before year end but not yet recorded, i.e., unrecorded accounts payable.

345. **Answer: A**

In auditing the completeness assertion for accounts payable, the auditor is concerned about the possible understatement of accounts payable. The appropriate population for a confirmation effort would, therefore, be vendors with whom the entity has previously done business, in order to try to identify unrecorded payables.

346. **Answer: A**

Performing substantive tests before the balance sheet date increases the risk that the auditor will not detect material misstatements in the balances at the balance sheet date. In selecting procedures to perform before the balance sheet date, the auditor must consider the problems involved in controlling this increase in risk. The auditor's primary concern with accounts payable is completeness. Confirmation efforts in this area would, therefore, be directed toward zero or low-balance accounts and would be least likely to be performed before the balance sheet date, as it would have to be re-performed as of the balance sheet date.

347. **Answer: C**

Vouching a sample of cash disbursements recorded just after year end to receiving reports and vendor invoices would enable the auditor to determine if the goods were actually received or owned before year end. As a result, the amounts paid after year end would need to be accrued as year-end liabilities.

348. **Answer: C**

Tracing a sample of purchase orders and the related receiving reports to the purchases journal and the cash disbursements journal will enable the auditor to determine that the purchases were properly recorded. Going from the detail into the records tests for the proper inclusion and recording of the items.

349. **Answer: C**

The permanent file would usually include copies or abstracts of significant contracts that affect multiple years. Lease agreements have financial statement effects and frequently involve multiple years, so the auditor would keep those copies or abstracts of key provisions in the permanent file.

350. **Answer: A**

The tickmark € is consistently used with respect to payments. Tracing those payments to the cash disbursements journal and then to the relevant bank statement is a relevant audit procedure to gather evidence as to the validity of identified payments of this debt.

351. **Answer: C**

The tickmark ¥ is consistently used with respect to 20X1 "expense." Calculating the interest expense (presumably using the effective interest method) is a relevant audit procedure to gather evidence as to the reasonableness of such recorded expense.

352. **Answer: C**

In auditing long-term bonds payable, an auditor would compare interest expense with the bond payable amount for reasonableness. This procedure would provide evidence supporting the completeness and proper statement of interest expense, including limited evidence related to the amortization of bond premium and discounts. It would also provide evidence supporting the completeness and proper statement of the bonds payable balance.

353. **Answer: C**

The primary responsibility of an independent registrar or stock transfer agent is to ensure that the stock issued by a corporation is in accordance with the capital stock provisions in the corporate charter and the authorization by the board of directors. Auditors confirm with them to determine whether any capital stock transactions have occurred and the accuracy of existing transactions, the effect of which is to confirm issued and outstanding shares.

354. **Answer: D**

Frequently, procedures that address presentation and disclosure also address rights and obligations. The rights and obligations assertion would relate to whether the entity had the rights to the reported retained earnings.

355. **Answer: A**

To verify stockholders' equity transactions, the auditor would review minutes of board of directors' meetings. The minutes would document changes such as the issuance of new capital stock, the purchase of treasury shares, or merger through an exchange of stock.

356. **Answer: D**

The review of payroll tax reconciliations is performed to identify potential liabilities for unpaid payroll taxes. The salaries and wages on which the payroll taxes are based are typically reconciled to gross salaries and wages per the general ledger. If the amounts differ, it may indicate additional payroll tax liabilities.

357. **Answer: D**

When control risk is assessed as low, substantive procedures in this area are typically limited to analytical procedures and recalculating year-end accruals.

358. **Answer: A**

The presence of significant unexplained variances between standard and actual labor costs might cause an auditor to suspect an employee payroll fraud scheme. The other choices provided represent internal control strengths in the payroll area.

359. **Answer: B**

The auditor evaluates an entity's costs and expenses to try to detect any material misstatements present. The best comparison would be current and prior year payroll expenses, as they are likely to be related to each other. Thus, prior year expense can be used to predict likely current year expense. If the numbers are materially different, this could indicate the existence of a material misstatement.

360. **Answer: B**

Fraud risk increases when copies of documents are provided instead of originals and more so when they are related to a single vendor, rather than multiple vendors. The auditor will need to obtain other evidence to support the transactions in question.

361. **Answer: B**

Nonsampling risk refers to any error unrelated to sampling risk that the auditor might commit when performing an audit sampling task, such as failing to recognize a misstatement or otherwise misinterpreting the audit evidence.

362. **Answer: B**

Both the expected amount of misstatements and the measure of tolerable misstatement are factors that would influence sample size for a substantive test of details for a specific account.

363. **Answer: D**

The use of statistical methods assists the auditor in designing an efficient sample, measuring the sufficiency of the evidence, and evaluating the sample results. Thus, this provides an objective basis for quantitatively evaluating sample risk.

364. **Answer: C**

Attribute sampling is used to reach a conclusion about a population in terms of a rate of occurrence (quantifiable).

365. **Answer: D**

Testing controls associated with granting credit to customers for sales on account would appropriately involve sampling (specifically, attributes sampling).

366. **Answer: B**

Population size is not considered in determining the sample size for an attributes sampling application. The tables that are used to determine the sample size for attributes sampling are based upon an assumption that the population is very, very large. Hence, an increase in the population size would have a negligible effect.

367. **Answer: A**

The term "attributes sampling" is used in the context of testing internal control issues, such as evaluating the appropriate authorization of purchase transactions.

368. **Answer: D**

In attributes sampling, the sample size is determined using available tables that do not explicitly consider population size. That is because the tables are based on an underlying assumption of very large population sizes. Accordingly, a change in population size has little impact on sample size.

369. **Answer: D**

The sample size of a test of controls varies inversely with the tolerable deviation rate. It varies directly with the expected population rate.

370. **Answer: B**

Incorrect acceptance involves concluding that a financial statement element was fairly stated, based on an audit sampling application, when, in fact, the element was materially misstated. This is consistent with the circumstances described in this question.

371. **Answer: C**

Variables sampling, or classical variables sampling, is used to calculate a best estimate of a population value with confidence intervals around the estimate. Commonly used variables sampling methods are mean-per-unit, difference estimation, and ratio estimation.

372. **Answer: A**

Ratio estimation is most efficient when the differences are proportional to book values. If the calculated audit amounts are approximately proportional to the book amounts, a correlation exists between book values and the individual differences, and ratio estimation will be effective.

373. **Answer: C**

Increasing tolerable misstatement decreases sample size, while increasing the assessed level of control risk increases sample size.

374. **Answer: B**

AICPA Professional Standards have described "projected misstatement" as the amount of known misstatements identified in a sample that is projected to the population from which the sample was drawn.

375. **Answer: A**

PPS sampling is most effective in detecting overstatements, since the likelihood of an item's selection increases with the recorded magnitude of the item.

376. **Answer: C**

When the recorded balance of the account involved is less than the sampling interval, the auditor must determine the "tainting" percentage and apply that percentage to the sampling interval. In this case the tainting percentage = [($5,000 − $1,000)/$5,000] = 80%. Accordingly, the projected misstatement is $6,000 × 80% = $4,800.

377. Answer: D

n = Reliability factor (from tables) × Book value   3 × $240,000 = 30

Tolerable misstatement, net of expected misstatements $24,000

378. Answer: B

In a probability-proportional-to-size application, the projected error of the sample is the amount of the difference between the book value and the audit value when the amount of the account examined is greater than the sampling interval.

As the selected account receivable was $10,000 and the sampling interval was $5,000, the projected error was $2,000 (the actual difference between the recorded amount and the audit value).

379. Answer: A

In an EDI system, a standard format is adopted. Mapping is the process by which the elements in the client's computer system are related to the standard data elements.

380. Answer: D

A disaster recovery plan is the entity's plan to restore and maintain operations in the event of a major disaster such as a flood, hurricane, or fire.

Storage of duplicate files in a separate location would enable a company to begin processing at a new site if the computer center were unusable.

381. Answer: A

When users fail to change their passwords, this presents a password security problem. It provides hackers with unlimited time in which to discover the password.

382. Answer: D

The auditor's objective is to collect sufficient evidence to express an opinion on the financial statements and to provide reasonable assurance that the financial statements are not materially misstated. Thus, the auditor's objective in assessing control risk is to determine how internal controls affect the risk that the financial statements will be materially misstated. Remember that control risk is the risk that internal controls will fail to prevent or detect a material misstatement.

383. Answer: B

Filtering data (i.e., screening based upon specified criteria) is something that generalized audit software is well suited to do.

384. Answer: C

Misstatements in a batch computer system caused by incorrect programs or data may not be detected immediately because there are time delays in processing transactions in a batch system. In a batch system, transactions are grouped together in batches and then processed.

385. Answer: A

Limit tests and validity check tests are both processing controls designed to ensure the reliability and accuracy of data processing. While the Study Text has included both as examples of input controls, they can also be utilized as processing controls.

386. Answer: B

Edit checks ensure that only valid transactions are processed. The direct output of edit checks for a sales order processing system would most likely be a file of all rejected sales transactions. These transactions would need to be researched and corrected so that they could be re-entered into processing.

387. Answer: C

A validity check is a check to see if the data carry valid values. Of the items listed, this item is the only validity check. The computer matches a control field value to an existing file record and highlights those which do not match.

388. Answer: B

Using computer-assisted audit techniques to match the Social Security numbers for all employees in the payroll transaction file to the population of government-authorized Social Security numbers would identify any employees having invalid Social Security numbers.

389. **Answer: A**

An advantage of computer-assisted audit techniques, such as IDEA or ACL, is the capability of analyzing very large (even entire) populations of data.

390. **Answer: B**

An embedded audit module is a program inserted into the client's system to capture designated transactions, such as large or unusual transactions, for later review by the auditor.

It enables the auditor to continuously test the client's computerized information system.

391. **Answer: D**

Parallel simulation is a computer-assisted auditing technique in which an auditor-written or auditor-controlled program is used to process client data. The results are then compared to those obtained using the client's program and differences are investigated.

This technique enables the auditor to test controls in and processing performed by a client program.

392. **Answer: D**

Embedded audit modules continuously monitor transaction activity and collect data on auditor-designated transactions. They must be inserted into the client's system and thus would require that the auditor be involved with the system design of the application to be monitored.

393. **Answer: B**

Significant deficiencies are control deficiencies, or combinations of control deficiencies, "such that there is a reasonable possibility that a material misstatement of the entity's financial statements will not be prevented, or detected and corrected, on a timely basis." If significant deficiencies are discovered as a result of the testing of internal controls, the audit must be modified to ensure that these deficiencies have not resulted in a material misstatement of the financial statements. The auditor would increase the control risk assessment and increase substantive testing.

394. **Answer: B**

"Test data" would not be helpful in evaluating physical security controls over unclaimed checks or other documents.

395. **Answer: A**

Electronic data interchange (EDI) utilizes standardized formats for electronically transferring information. By adopting EDI, a company can electronically transfer information from one system into another. The elimination of manual re-entry of data and paperwork reduces costs and increases accuracy.

396. **Answer: D**

Parallel simulation is a computer-assisted auditing technique in which an auditor-written or auditor-controlled program is used to process client data. The results are then compared to those obtained using the client's program and differences are investigated. This technique enables the auditor to test controls in and processing performed by a client program.

397. **Answer: C**

A Trojan horse involves the inclusion of unauthorized programming in an otherwise legitimate program. They are frequently included in "free" software downloadable from Internet sites. For example, free software made available to AOL subscribers included special instructions that secretly forwarded the subscriber's account name and password to another party.

398. **Answer: A**

In an EDI system, a standard format is adopted. Mapping is the process by which the elements in the client's computer system are related to the standard data elements.

399. **Answer: A**

Network and sender/recipient acknowledgments document the trail of accounting data (and transactions) through the system. In doing so, they serve as essential elements of the audit trail in an EDI system.

400. Answer: C

When the predecessor considers reissuing an audit report, the predecessor should read the current auditor's (successor's) report and compare it to the predecessor's report. The predecessor should obtain a representation letter from the successor auditor addressing any matters known to the successor that are relevant to the predecessor's previously issued report.

401. Answer: C

The objective is to prevent users of audited financial statements from misinterpreting the degree of responsibility the auditor is assuming when the auditor's name is associated with financial statements.

402. Answer: B

In order to issue an unmodified opinion, the auditor must be confident that no material misstatements exist in the financial statements. While misstatements may exist, in total they must be believed to be less than a material amount.

403. Answer: A

PCAOB auditing standards require that such a statement regarding the auditor's tenure be expressed somewhere within the audit report, not in Form AP.

404. Answer: B

The PCAOB requires the auditor's report to be dated at the point at which the auditor obtained sufficient appropriate audit evidence as a basis for the opinion. The date of the audit report is unrelated to when the company files its financial statements with the SEC.

405. Answer: B

The identification of a critical audit matter is the responsibility of the auditor, and no response is required from the issuer's audit committee regarding agreement or disagreement with the auditor's judgment in that regard.

406. Answer: C

When part of the audit is performed by a component auditor, the group auditor is required to make inquiries concerning the professional reputation, independence, and competence of the component auditor.

407. Answer: C

AICPA Professional Standards, specifically *Terms of Engagement* (AU-C 210.A26), identify five considerations that may influence the decision to obtain a separate engagement letter under these circumstances: (1) who engages the component auditor; (2) whether a separate auditor's report is to be issued on the component; (3) legal requirements regarding the appointment of the auditor; (4) the degree of ownership by the parent; and (5) the degree of independence of the component management from the parent entity. The turnover of the component's board members is not a relevant consideration.

408. Answer: A

The auditor should express an unmodified opinion. The disclosure of the contingent liability has been made and is considered adequate by the auditor.

An emphasis-of-matter paragraph may be added after the opinion paragraph to bring attention to the uncertainty.

409. Answer: D

An unmodified audit report would be appropriate, since there is no need for disclosure if the likelihood of a material loss is indeed remote.

410. Answer: A

If the auditor is unable to obtain the audited financial statements of a significant subsidiary, the auditor has a scope limitation. As a result, a qualified or disclaimer opinion would be expressed (and an unmodified opinion would be inappropriate).

411. Answer: B

The last sentence in the Auditor's Responsibility section would be modified to state, "We believe that the audit evidence we have obtained is sufficient and appropriate to provide a basis for our qualified audit opinion." A qualified opinion resulting from a scope limitation (an insufficiency of audit evidence) also results in the addition of a separate paragraph (Basis for Qualified Opinion, which describes the circumstances involved) and a modified opinion paragraph. No mention would be made in the notes to the financial statements.

412. **Answer: C**

When an entity omits a statement of cash flows, the auditor may accept an engagement to audit the other financial statements, but should qualify the opinion, since a statement of cash flows is required when general-purpose financial statements present financial position and results of operation.

413. **Answer: D**

An opinion qualified because of inadequate disclosure would include a separate basis for qualified opinion paragraph describing the nature of the omission and modifications in the opinion paragraph. There would be no modifications in the introductory or management responsibility paragraphs.

414. **Answer: D**

When a misstatement is material and the effect on the financial statements is pervasive, the auditor should express an adverse opinion indicating that the financial statements are not fairly stated.

415. **Answer: D**

An unjustified change in accounting principles is a GAAP departure that would result in a qualified or adverse opinion. A material weakness in internal control should be reported to those charged with governance, but would not be reported in an unmodified audit report.

416. **Answer: C**

A disclaimer is issued when the scope limitations pertaining to the audit are so pervasive that the auditor in unable to express an opinion. Lack of adequate disclosures in the financial statements is a GAAP departure, not a scope limitation. Thus, a disclaimer of opinion would not be appropriate.

417. **Answer: B**

Morris should disclaim an opinion because of the pervasiveness of the scheme and the nature of the items involved.

Although the auditor was not precluded by the client from obtaining sufficient evidence to evaluate the impact of the illegal bribes on the financial statements, the fact that they could not ascertain whether senior management was involved is a critical deficiency.

418. **Answer: D**

A disclaimer report omits the scope paragraph (the second paragraph in the auditor's responsibility section that describes an audit) and adds a separate paragraph explaining why the audit did not comply with generally accepted auditing standards (Basis for Disclaimer of Opinion). The scope paragraph is omitted because any descriptions of procedures performed could be misunderstood. If a disclaimer is issued, the auditor does not feel that the audit work performed was sufficient to render an opinion. The opinion paragraph remains but it indicates that the scope of work was insufficient to support an opinion.

419. **Answer: A**

The auditor's report should not mention a change in accounting principle that has an immaterial effect on comparability. Only material matters are relevant to the auditor's report.

420. **Answer: C**

A change in depreciation method applicable to existing assets would be viewed as a change in estimate, not a change in accounting principle. (In this case, the different depreciation method is only applicable to new assets, which would not even be considered a change in estimate.) In any case, since the effect on the current period's financial statements is specified to be immaterial, an unmodified opinion should be expressed.

421. **Answer: A**

When there is a change in accounting principle, the auditor is required to evaluate four matters: (1) whether the newly adopted principle is GAAP; (2) whether the method of accounting for the effect of the change conforms to GAAP; (3) whether the disclosures related to the change are adequate; and (4) whether the company has justified that the alternative accounting principle is GAAP. Hence, it is not true to suggest that the change must be authorized by those charged with governance.

422. Answer: A

When there is a change in accounting principle, the auditor should evaluate whether: (1) the newly adopted principle is GAAP; (2) the method of accounting for the effect of the change conforms to GAAP; (3) the disclosures related to the change are adequate; and (4) the company has justified that the alternative accounting principle is preferable. If one (or more) of the above criteria is (are) not met, the auditor should treat the matter, if material, as a GAAP departure, which involves a choice between a qualified opinion and an adverse opinion.

423. Answer: B

PCAOB auditing standards (specifically, AS Section 2820) identify two specific matters that affect the auditor's evaluation of consistency of financial statements: (1) a change in accounting principle; and (2) an adjustment to correct a misstatement in previously issued financial statements (i.e., a "restatement"). A change in accounting principle may be at management's discretion or it may be mandated by a change in accounting standards that eliminates an accounting alternative that was previously accepted but no longer is.

424. Answer: A

When there is such an inconsistency the auditor should evaluate whether (1) the adopted principle is in accordance with the applicable financial reporting framework; (2) whether the effect of the change is accounted for in accordance with the applicable reporting framework; (3) whether disclosures about the change are adequate; and (4) whether the entity has justified that the alternative selected is preferable.

425. Answer: D

The auditor may inquire of the predecessor auditor about issues related to the consistency of financial reporting over time, but that is not something that the auditor is required to inquire about prior to accepting the audit engagement. The other answer options should be conducted prior to acceptance.

AICPA Professional Standards require an auditor (the successor) to make several inquiries of the predecessor auditor before accepting the audit engagement. These

matters include: (1) information bearing on the integrity of management; (2) disagreements with management about accounting or auditing issues; (3) communications to those charged with governance about fraud and noncompliance with laws and regulations; (4) communications to management and those charged with governance about internal control issues; and (5) the predecessor's understanding for the reasons the entity changed auditors.

426. Answer: D

When the audited financial statements are presented in a client's document containing other information, the auditor is required to read the other information to determine whether it is consistent with the audited financial statements.

427. Answer: C

When an auditor has been engaged to determine whether supplementary information is fairly stated in relation to the financial statements, the auditor may include in the auditor's report on the financial statements an opinion that the accompanying information is fairly stated in all material respects in relation to the financial statements as a whole.

428. Answer: A

The accountant's separate report on the supplementary information should include a statement that the supplementary information is the responsibility of management and was derived from and relates directly to the underlying records used to prepare the financial statements. The report should further state that the supplementary information was not audited or reviewed (since it was compiled) and that no assurance of any type is provided.

429. Answer: A

The auditor should make certain specific inquiries of management about the required supplementary information, including (1) whether it is measured and presented in accordance with prescribed guidelines; (2) whether the methods of measurement or presentation have been changed relative to the prior period; and (3) whether any significant assumptions affect the measurement or presentation of it.

430. **Answer: D**

AICPA Professional Standards describe the limited procedures that the auditor is to perform to address required supplementary information. The auditor is further required to report deficiencies in or the omission of such information.

431. **Answer: A**

Information that a company voluntarily presents on its web site is outside the PCAOB's definition of "supplemental information." As a practical matter, sustainability reports are not required, nor is third-party assurance on sustainability required.

432. **Answer: B**

The auditor should obtain management's representation that the methods of measurement or presentation have not changed from those used in the prior period. However, the auditor's report does not include such a statement.

433. **Answer: D**

The alert to restrict the distribution of the auditor's report is presented at the end of the auditor's report.

434. **Answer: D**

Provided that the financial statements prepared in conformity with another country's GAAP are for use only outside the United States, KCP America's auditor may issue either a U.S.-style report revised to reference the accounting principles (financial reporting framework) of the parent's country or the report form of the parent's country.

435. **Answer: A**

When reporting on financial statements prepared in conformity with another country's accounting principles, an auditor practicing in the U.S. must perform the procedures necessary to comply with the professional standards of U.S. generally accepted auditing standards. The auditor must understand the accounting principles generally accepted in the other country.

436. **Answer: A**

An auditor's report on condensed financial statements should indicate:

1) the auditor has audited and expressed an opinion on the complete financial statements;

2) the date of the auditor's report on such statements;

3) the type of opinion expressed; and

4) whether the information in the condensed financial statements is consistent, in all material respects, with the audited financial statements.

437. **Answer: D**

The professional standards indicate that in order to perform a review of interim financial information, the accountant should have an understanding of the entity's business and its internal control as they relate to the preparation of both annual and interim financial information sufficient to identify potential material misstatements and to select appropriate inquiry and analytical procedures.

438. **Answer: C**

The AICPA's sample management representation letter for interim financial information does not include a representation about understanding the meaning of a "review" of interim financial information. The nature of such an engagement would be clearly communicated in the required engagement letter, but it would not be a statement of fact by management in response to the auditor's inquiries.

439. **Answer: A**

An accountant's report on the application of accounting principles to a specific transaction should include: 1) a statement that the engagement was conducted in accordance with applicable AICPA standards, 2) a description of the transaction and the accounting principles to be applied, 3) a statement indicating that responsibility for proper accounting treatment rests with the preparers of the financial statements, and 4) a statement that any difference in the facts, circumstances, or assumptions may change the report. (AU 625)

440. **Answer: B**

The auditor's report should include the word "independent," regardless of the financial reporting framework used in preparing the entity's financial statements.

441. **Answer: A**

The financial statements would contain a footnote that describes the basis of the financial statement presentation and how it differs from GAAP.

442. **Answer: D**

The auditor may express an opinion on a single financial statement (such as the balance sheet) and this is consistent with the meaning of the phrase "taken as a whole." Of course, the auditor must still obtain sufficient appropriate evidence as a reasonable basis for that opinion.

443. **Answer: C**

When an auditor is engaged to audit a specific element of the financial statements, i.e., selected financial data, in conjunction with an engagement to audit the financial statements, the report on the specific element should include the date of the audit report on the financial statements and the type of opinion expressed.

444. **Answer: C**

Special reports apply to engagements that involve compliance with contracts or regulatory requirements related to financial statements.

445. **Answer: C**

When commenting on compliance with contractual requirements in an audit report on an entity's financial statements, the commentary about compliance should be presented in an other-matter paragraph that follows the opinion paragraph on the financial statements.

446. **Answer: B**

The "subject matter" attestation standards also require compliance with other relevant attestation standards, including AT-C 105, *Concepts Common to All Attestation Engagements*. AT-C 105.27 states that the engagement should be accepted only when all personnel performing the engagement have the necessary competence and capabilities.

447. **Answer: A**

The user auditor should plan to read the service auditor's report, whether on controls placed in operation (type 1 report) or on operating effectiveness (type 2 report) in connection with obtaining an understanding of internal controls at the service organization that may be relevant to the user entity's financial statements.

448. **Answer: D**

This question focuses on matters that are relevant to the service auditor's report on internal controls at the service organization. Of the answer choices, this is the only one that involves a procedure that is actually performed at the service organization, so it would be relevant to the service auditor's engagement.

449. **Answer: A**

A report on controls placed in operation should include a disclaimer on operating effectiveness as this type of engagement does not include any tests of controls. It is not intended to provide a user auditor with a basis for reducing control risk below maximum.

450. **Answer: D**

Comfort letters are requested by and addressed to underwriters and other parties. They provide the underwriter with "reasonable grounds to believe there are no material omissions or misstatements in financial statements related to a 1933 Act securities offering." They are addressed to the underwriter (or other requesting parties) and signed by the auditor.

451. **Answer: A**

Comfort letters are issued (and signed) by an entity's independent auditor for the purpose of providing a "due diligence" defense to underwriters and certain other requesting parties in connection with a securities offering.

452. **Answer: A**

When auditing a governmental entity under the Single Audit Act, the auditor should perform the engagement both in accordance with GAAS and in accordance with Generally Accepted Government Auditing Standards that impose several additional audit requirements.

453. **Answer: D**

In a governmental audit, the auditor has the choice of issuing a combined audit and internal control report or issuing separate reports.

454. **Answer: B**

Auditors are required to report known or likely fraud, illegal acts, violations of contracts or grants, or abuse directly to outside parties when: (1) management fails to report such information as required by law or regulation; or (2) management fails to take timely and appropriate action to respond to fraud, illegal acts, violations, or abuse that is likely to be material to the financial statements and involves government agency funding.

455. **Answer: B**

If the material noncompliance occurred subsequent to the period associated with the audit report, the auditor would not modify the opinion.

456. **Answer: D**

The OMB's Uniform Grant Guidance (which encompasses the former Circular A-133) defines a subrecipient as "a non-Federal entity that receives a subaward from a pass-through entity to carry out part of a Federal program." In other words, a subrecipient is an entity that expends awards received from another entity to carry out a federal program.

457. **Answer: B**

"Must" indicates an unconditional requirement in the SSARSs.

458. **Answer: D**

The Statements on Standards for Accounting and Review Services are not applicable when: 1) preparing a working trial balance; 2) assisting in adjusting the books of account; 3) consulting on accounting, tax, and similar matters; 4) preparing tax returns; 5) providing bookkeeping or data processing services, and 6) processing financial data for clients of other accounting firms.

459. **Answer: A**

AR-C 70 does, in fact, apply to engagements to prepare financial statements to be presented alongside a personal financial plan. However, AR-C 70 does not apply to an engagement to prepare financial statements as part of a written personal financial plan prepared by the accountant. The key word here is "alongside" a personal financial plan.

460. **Answer: A**

There is nothing in the applicable AICPA Professional Standards (specifically, AR-C section 80, *Compilation Engagements*) that would prevent an accountant from accepting an engagement to compile an entity's current year financial statements as well as the prior year's financial statements (even though the prior year's financial statements had been compiled by a predecessor accountant whose report has not been reissued).

461. **Answer: D**

In general, the accountant who compiles such financial statements must believe that the omission of the disclosures is not undertaken for the purpose of misleading readers of those financial statements.

462. **Answer: D**

A compilation engagement carries no expectation that the accountant will obtain an understanding of the entity's internal control. There would be no such review of the entity's segregation of duties.

463. **Answer: C**

The term "other-matter paragraph" applies to topics that are not reported in the financial statements, such as the accountant's role in the review engagement or other engagement-related issues.

464. **Answer: C**

An emphasis-of-matter paragraph addresses an issue that is already properly identified in the financial statements of the entity. GAAP requires disclosure of significant transactions with related parties, so it is likely that the practitioner would choose to comment further on those related party issues.

465. **Answer: A**

It may be permissible to change an engagement from an audit to a review. The review report should include a sentence stating that "A review is substantially less in scope than an audit ..."

466. **Answer: A**

The basis for conclusions in a review engagement consists primarily of inquiries and analytical procedures. An analytical procedure such as this might be performed.

467. **Answer: A**

In these circumstances, AICPA standards require the accountant to add a separate paragraph to the review report stating (1) that the prior period's financial statements were audited; (2) the date of the previous report; (3) the type of opinion expressed; (4) the reasons for any modification of the report; and (5) that no auditing procedures were performed after the date of the previous report.

468. **Answer: B**

AICPA Professional Standards related to compilation of pro forma financial information point out that the accountant is not prohibited from issuing a compilation report under those circumstances, but the compilation report should disclose the lack of independence.

469. **Answer: C**

When the current-period financial statements have been reviewed and the prior period financial statements were audited, the accountant's review report on the current period should indicate the degree of responsibility assumed for the prior financials. The current report would include a separate (other-matter) paragraph indicating, among other things, that no auditing procedures were performed after the date of the 20x1 auditor's report.

470. **Answer: D**

The auditor's report should not be dated prior to the date on which the auditor has obtained sufficient appropriate audit evidence as a reasonable basis for the auditor's opinion.

471. **Answer: C**

A "top-down approach" begins at the financial statement level; uses the auditor's evaluation of overall risks to internal control over financial reporting; considers entity-level controls; considers significant account balances, disclosures, and their relevant assertions; and so on. It begins at the financial statement level and works down to the relevant assertion level to select relevant controls for testing.

472. **Answer: C**

The term "entity-level control" refers to those policies and procedures that have very broad implications to the achievement of an entity's control-related objectives related to operating activities, financial reporting, and compliance. However, the entity's control objectives would not generally be applicable to a company's annual stockholder meeting.

473. **Answer: D**

When issuing a separate audit report on the financial statements and on internal control over financial reporting, the separate reports should each contain an additional paragraph that references the other report.

474. **Answer: D**

AS Section 6115 states that such an engagement is voluntary.

475. **Answer: B**

PCAOB auditing standards (specifically, Section 2201, para. 20) state: "In planning the audit of internal control over financial reporting, the auditor should use the same materiality considerations he or she would use in planning the audit of the company's annual financial statements."

476. **Answer: A**

The Uniform Commercial Code focuses on sales laws and other commercial transactions, not employee benefit plans.

477. **Answer: A**

The auditor's report references the statements of net assets available for benefits and the related statement of changes in net assets available for benefits.

478. **Answer: C**

A compilation does not involve any form of assurance at all.

479. **Answer: B**

Statements on Standards for Attestation Engagements apply specifically to an attest engagement performed by a CPA. That is defined as examining, reviewing, or performing agreed-upon procedures on subject matter or an assertion by the responsible party about the subject matter. The engagement described here is an examination (resulting in the expression of opinion) on management's assertion about the square footage of a warehouse.

480. **Answer: C**

Independence is an important quality control consideration for engagements that involve assurance, including agreed-upon procedures engagements (which express assurance in the form of "procedures" and "findings").

481. **Answer: B**

The engagement letter should not specify the practitioner's threshold for determining what is "material" to the engagement.

482. **Answer: D**

The clue here is that the CPA was engaged to examine management's assertion. An engagement of this nature is addressed by the Statements on Standards for Attestation Engagements. Attestation engagements are "engagement is defined as follows: "An examination, review, or agreed-upon procedures engagement performed under the attestation standards related to subject matter or an assertion that is the responsibility of another party.""

483. **Answer: C**

The practitioner should express an adverse opinion when the subject matter is misstated in a way that is material and pervasive.

484. **Answer: B**

When a misstatement of the subject matter is material, but NOT pervasive, the practitioner should express a qualified opinion. When expressing either a qualified or an adverse opinion due to misstatement of the subject matter, the practitioner should express the opinion directly on the subject matter.

485. **Answer: A**

When the engaging party is the responsible party and refuses to provide a written assertion, the practitioner should withdraw from the engagement, assuming that is allowed by law.

486. **Answer: A**

When the engaging party is the responsible party and refuses to provide the requested written representations, the practitioner should withdraw from the engagement, assuming that is allowed by law.

487. **Answer: C**

The review report should include a statement that a review is substantially less in scope than an examination, and a disclaimer of opinion should be included.

488. **Answer: C**

The practitioner should not refer to an external specialist when the practitioner's review report is unmodified. When expressing a modified conclusion and reference to the external specialist may be helpful to readers in understanding the reason for the modification, the practitioner's review report may refer to the external specialist. However, there is no requirement to restrict the distribution of the report.

489. **Answer: A**

The practitioner's agreed-upon procedures report should state that the procedures were agreed to by the specified parties.

490. **Answer: A**

An agreed-upon procedures report expresses assurance in the form of procedures and findings with respect to the procedures performed.

491. **Answer: B**

If the practitioner is unable to obtain sufficient appropriate evidence regarding the prospective financial statements, the practitioner should disclaim an opinion (and describe the scope limitation in the report).

492. **Answer: C**

When the underlying assumptions do not provide a reasonable basis for the prospective financial statements, the practitioner should issue an adverse opinion.

493. **Answer: D**

An accountant's report on a review of pro forma financial information should include a reference to the financial statements from which the historical financial information is derived and a statement as to whether such statements were audited or reviewed. Any modification of the report on the historical financial statements should also be identified.

494. **Answer: B**

When a practitioner does not have the necessary understanding of the client's business and industry for purposes of reporting on pro forma financial information, the practitioner should consider whether sufficient knowledge of these matters can be obtained. It is possible that industry-related knowledge might be obtained by reviewing applicable industry trade journals.

495. **Answer: C**

When the auditor issues separate reports on internal control over financial reporting and on compliance with applicable laws and regulations, each report should include a separate paragraph that references the other report.

496. **Answer: B**

An agreed-upon procedures engagement results in the issuance of a report that identifies the procedures performed and the results obtained. The report would include a list of the procedures performed (or reference thereto) and the findings.

497. **Answer: B**

The attestation standards must be followed when reviewing MD&A prepared pursuant to SEC requirements. The standards apply to both an examination and a review of MD&A.

498. **Answer: C**

This answer is correct because the professional standards provide for both review and examinations of MD&A.

499. **Answer: E**

This answer is correct because the attestation standards on MD&A do not include an assertion for rights and obligations. Those standards indicate that the four standards are completeness, consistency with the financial statements, occurrence, and presentation and disclosure.

500. **Answer: D**

In a WebTrust assurance engagement, the practitioner expresses an opinion on management's assertions regarding business practices, transaction integrity, and information protection. The engagement is conducted in accordance with the attestation standards. A WebTrust Seal of Assurance can be displayed for a limited period of time on the websites of entities who receive unqualified opinions in WebTrust engagements.

Task-Based Simulations

Ethics, Professional Responsibilities, and General Principles

AICPA Code of Professional Conduct: Members in Public Practice

MIPPs Independence Rules: Family Relationships

Task-Based Simulation 1

tbs.fam.relations.001_2017

Research		
	Authoritative Literature	
		Help

Situation:

Your accounting firm wants to hire Burt to join your audit group. Burt has a big family and you don't want to create any independence issues. Therefore, you examine Burt's situation carefully.

Required:

Answer the following questions selecting "yes" or "no" as appropriate.

	Yes	No
1. You want to put Burt on the audit team for the ABC Co. audit. Burt's sister is an officer of ABC. For AICPA Code purposes, is she an immediate family member (IFM)?	○	○
2. You want to put Burt on the audit team for the DEF Co. audit. His mother is a secretary at DEF. Is she a close relative for Code purposes?	○	○
3. You want to put Burt on the audit team for the GHI Co. audit. Burt's mother owns 3% of GHI's stock and his wife owns 3%. Is this an independence problem?	○	○
4. You want to put Burt on the audit team for the JKL Co. audit. Burt's dependent son is a new delivery boy at JKL. Does this create an independence problem?	○	○
5. You want to put Burt on the MNO Co. audit team. Burt's sister, unbeknownst to Burt, owns a big enough stake in MNO stock to be material to her but not enough to exercise significant influence over the audit client. Would this situation create an independence problem?	○	○

Answers and Explanations

Task-Based Simulation 1 Solution

Research

Authoritative Literature

Help

		Yes	No
1.	You want to put Burt on the audit team for the ABC Co. audit. Burt's sister is an officer of ABC. For AICPA Code purposes, is she an immediate family member (IFM)?	○	●
2.	You want to put Burt on the audit team for the DEF Co. audit. His mother is a secretary at DEF. Is she a close relative for Code purposes?	●	○
3.	You want to put Burt on the audit team for the GHI Co. audit. Burt's mother owns 3% of GHI's stock and his wife owns 3%. Is this an independence problem?	●	○
4.	You want to put Burt on the audit team for the JKL Co. audit. Burt's dependent son is a new delivery boy at JKL. Does this create an independence problem?	○	●
5.	You want to put Burt on the MNO Co. audit team. Burt's sister, unbeknownst to Burt, owns a big enough stake in MNO stock to be material to her but not enough to exercise significant influence over the audit client. Would this situation create an independence problem?	○	●

1. **No.** Only if she were a dependent of Burt would she be an IFM. That seems unlikely, since she is a corporate officer. That makes her a close relative.
2. **Yes.** she is. She would be an IFM only if she was dependent on Burt and the facts do not give any indication that this is the case.
3. **Yes.** Independence would be impaired because Burt's wife is an immediate family member (IFM) and owns stock in the audit client. An immediate family member cannot own any stock directly in Burt's audit client. Burt's mother is only a close relative and so her ownership would not impair independence.
4. **No.** This is the sort of job that even an IFM of an audit team member could have without creating a suspicious situation.
5. **No.** Only if the sister's financial stake is one that Burt knows or has reason to know is material to the sister or enables the sister to exercise significant influence over MNO would we have an independence problem.

Assessing Risk and Developing a Planned Response

Planning Activities

Audit Risk

Task-Based Simulation 2

tbs.AUDDocrev001

Research		
	Authoritative Literature	
		Help

A CPA firm is involved in the risk assessment and audit planning of the year 5 audit of ABA Company, a calendar year-end issuer. Your firm's new affiliated offshore entity sent you ABA's working trial balance and a related exhibit of ratios. Personnel from that entity also have provided a number of observations relating to significant changes between years 4 and 5 (unaudited) and certain suggested audit procedures based on the working trial balance.

As the audit senior for this engagement, it is your responsibility to review the document provided by the employees of the offshore entity. The materiality for the audit has, at this point, been set at $55,000.

To revise the risk assessment analysis, select the needed correction, if any, from the list provided. If the underlined text is already correct in the context of the document, select [Original Text] from the list. If removal of the entire underlined text is the best revision to the document as a whole, select [Delete Text] from the list.

ABA Company Note
Accounts Receivable Write-off
November 17, year 4

It is time we write off the $12,000 receivable from Gurley and Company for the sale this past March. We've tried to collect the account, but Gurley is in extremely dire financial condition. If we do recover it later, we can then charge some sort of miscellaneous income account.

Will Gent
Collections

Account #	Account	12/31/year 4			12/31/year 5 (unaudited)		% Change
	Working Trial Balance						
		Debit	**Credit**		**Debit**	**Credit**	
1000.10	Cash--First Natl. Bank	45,969			25,819		-78.0%
1050.10	Accounts receivable--trade	7,303,342			8,728,108		16.3%
1040.90	Allowance for bad debts		81,600			69,600	-17.2%
1100.10	Inventories	11,049,401			14,169,460		22.0%
1300.10	Prepaid expenses	133,365			149,988		11.1%
2050.00	Furniture, fixtures, office equipment	927,039			1,121,640		17.3%
2050.90	Accumulated depreciation		206,819			337,356	38.7%
2060.00	Leasehold improvements	84,065			84,065		0.0%
2060.90	Amortization of leasehold improvements		6,520			13,040	50.0%
2100.00	Software development cost	-			223,200		100.0%
2200.00	Intangible assets	850,000			680,000		-25.0%
3050.10	Accounts payable--trade		2,147,463			5,214,678	58.8%
3100.00	Capital lease obligations--current		36,720			46,524	21.1%
3210.10	Accrued liabilities		152,065			172,933	12.1%
3400.50	Line of credit--current		5,620,668			7,372,244	23.8%
4400.10	Capital lease obligations--noncurrent		388,195			360,128	-7.8%
5050.10	Capital stock		170,000			170,000	0.0%
5100.10	Paid-in capital		359,975			359,975	0.0%
5700.10	Retained earnings		10,382,273			11,223,156	7.5%
5900.00	Dividends	-			352,750	-	-
6000.10	Sales		81,990,631			78,698,143	-4.2%
7020.10	Cost of sales	63,004,070			61,314,381		-2.8%
7070.10	Salaries--sales	2,692,706			2,350,825		-14.5%
7070.50	Payroll benefits--sales	776,438			728,763		-6.5%
7075.10	Advertising & promotion	1,020,668			1,332,706		23.4%
7080.10	Travel & entertainment	518,320			378,760		-36.8%
7080.30	Miscellaneous expense--sales	284,657			236,858		-20.2%
7090.10	Salaries--operations	4,147,065			3,657,909		-13.4%
7090.30	Salaries--administrative	3,599,099			3,353,820		-7.3%
7090.50	Payroll benefits--admin.	1,540,492			1,692,557		9.0%
7100.10	Rent	678,130			613,143		-10.6%
7140.10	Utilities	178,921			199,613		10.4%
7200.10	Insurance	303,357			321,875		5.8%
7260.30	Legal & accounting	388,940			412,902		5.8%
7320.10	Bad debt expense	199,325			205,222		2.9%
7410.10	Supplies	472,893			407,065		-16.2%
7600.10	Depreciation and amort.	284,380			312,687		9.1%
7650.10	Software development cost	245,735			293,798		16.4%
7700.10	Miscellaneous exp.--administrative	199,373			208,638		4.4%
7800.10	Interest expense	358,142			405,364		11.6%
7900.10	Current income taxes	218,250			68,085		-220.6%
7900.70	Deferred income taxes	38,787			7,778		-398.7%
		101,542,928	**101,542,928**		**104,037,777**	**104,037,777**	2.4%
	Ratios						
	Current Ratio	2.32			1.80		
	Quick Ratio	0.92			0.68		
	AR Turnover (using ending AR)	11.23			9.02		
	Inventory Turnover (using ending Inv.)	8.63			7.02		
	Days Sales in Ending Inventory	42.31			51.96		
	Gross Margin Percentage	0.23			0.22		
	Net Income	840,883.75			195,395.45		

Email from CFO

From: CFO@ABA.com
Sent: June 23, year 4, 3:32 PM
To: Controller@ABA.com

Subject: Software Development Costs

We are in the process of developing device software that will make it much easier for our customers to integrate the use of our products. We are very early in the process and hope that this will significantly help us to increase our overall sales. This seems particularly important to us since our total sales (dollars and per unit) have decreased this year.

We should capitalize these costs; amortization of the costs should not begin until we have a marketable product. In the event this doesn't work out, I will inform you and we will write off the accumulated costs at that point.

TO: US ABA Company Audit Team

FROM: Offshore Audit Entity

RE: Risk Assessment Analysis

DATE: January 7, year 6

We have formatted the ABA Company working trial balance into that of the CPA firm and have calculated the various ratios requested. Following are areas we believe include significant changes between years and our tentative explanations.

The ABA Company experienced a major decrease in earnings, with this year's unaudited results decreasing to less than $200,000 as compared to last year's audited results of well over $840,000.

	(A)	(B)	(C)	(D)	(E)	(F)
1. Sales decreased during the year and the gross margin percentage decreased slightly, which is consistent with the A. existence of fixed costs in cost of sales. B. [Delete Text] C. increase in accounts receivable. D. increase in inventories. E. payment of dividends, whereas none had been paid in year 4. F. Decrease in travel and entertainment expense.	○	○	○	○	○	○
2. The current ratio decreased in large part due to an A. increase in inventory and accounts receivable. B. [Delete Text] C. Increase in accounts payable and the line of credit. D. Increase in utilities and insurance. E. Decrease in accounts receivable. F. Increase in the allowance for doubtful accounts.	○	○	○	○	○	○

(Continued)

	(A)	(B)	(C)	(D)	(E)	(F)
3. A large part of the quick ratio's decrease is due to	○	○	○	○	○	○

3. A large part of the quick ratio's decrease is due to
   A. the 78% decrease in cash.
   B. [Delete Text]
   C. amortization of leasehold improvements.
   D. a decrease in capital lease obligations—noncurrent
   E. an increase in inventories.
   F. an increase in accounts payable.

4. The decrease in AR turnover may indicate a(n) ○ ○ ○ ○ ○ ○
   A. increased risk of future bad debts.
   B. [Delete Text]
   C. decreased risk of future declines in sales.
   D. need to consider the completeness of recording of accounts receivable.
   E. need to consider whether sales made shortly after year-end were not included in year-end accounts receivable.
   F. provide additional disclosures with respect to consignment sales.

5. In addition, we recommend the following audit procedures: ○ ○ ○ ○ ○ ○
   A. Vouch changes in net leasehold improvements by comparing purchase and sales invoices with recorded entries.
   B. [Delete Text]
   C. Observe the physical count of leasehold improvements.
   D. Compare retirements of leasehold improvements as recorded with item itself.
   E. Determine that title has passed to the client on the year's acquisitions.

6. Because the allowance for bad debts decreased while accounts receivable increased, we should examine cash collections ○ ○ ○ ○ ○ ○
   A. shortly before year-end
   B. [Delete Text]
   C. shortly after year-end
   D. from throughout the year
   E. on related party receivables paid during the year and age year-end accounts receivable.

7. Based on the information provided, we should address whether the amounts capitalized as software development ○ ○ ○ ○ ○ ○
   A. include all direct and indirect costs involved.
   B. [Delete Text]
   C. are presented at their expected net realizable values.
   D. are properly capitalizable or period expenses.
   E. properly reflect related product liability costs.

Answers and Explanations

Task-Based Simulation 2 Solution

Research

Authoritative Literature

Help

	(A)	(B)	(C)	(D)	(E)	(F)
1. Sales decreased during the year and the gross margin percentage decreased slightly, which is consistent with the A. existence of fixed costs in cost of sales. B. [Delete Text] C. increase in accounts receivable. D. increase in inventories. E. payment of dividends, whereas none had been paid in year 4. F. Decrease in travel and entertainment expense.	●	○	○	○	○	○
2. The current ratio decreased in large part due to an A. increase in inventory and accounts receivable. B. [Delete Text] C. Increase in accounts payable and the line of credit. D. Increase in utilities and insurance. E. Decrease in accounts receivable. F. Increase in the allowance for doubtful accounts.	○	○	●	○	○	○
3. A large part of the quick ratio's decrease is due to A. the 78% decrease in cash. B. [Delete Text] C. amortization of leasehold improvements. D. a decrease in capital lease obligations—noncurrent E. an increase in inventories. F. an increase in accounts payable.	○	○	○	○	○	●
4. The decrease in AR turnover may indicate a(n) A. increased risk of future bad debts. B. [Delete Text] C. decreased risk of future declines in sales. D. need to consider the completeness of recording of accounts receivable. E. need to consider whether sales made shortly after year-end were not included in year-end accounts receivable. F. provide additional disclosures with respect to consignment sales.	●	○	○	○	○	○
5. In addition, we recommend the following audit procedures: A. Vouch changes in net leasehold improvements by comparing purchase and sales invoices with recorded entries. B. [Delete Text] C. Observe the physical count of leasehold improvements. D. Compare retirements of leasehold improvements as recorded with item itself. E. Determine that title has passed to the client on the year's acquisitions.	○	●	○	○	○	○

(Continued)

	(A)	(B)	(C)	(D)	(E)	(F)
6. Because the allowance for bad debts decreased while accounts receivable increased, we should examine cash collections A. shortly before year-end B. [Delete Text] C. shortly after year-end D. from throughout the year E. on related party receivables paid during the year and age year-end accounts receivable.	○	○	●	○	○	○
7. Based on the information provided, we should address whether the amounts capitalized as software development A. include all direct and indirect costs involved. B. [Delete Text] C. are presented at their expected net realizable values. D. are properly capitalizable or period expenses. E. properly reflect related product liability costs.	○	○	○	●	○	○

1. **(A)** Gross margin decreased from .23 to .22. Because any fixed costs will be spread over less units of items, this is consistent with a lesser decrease in the cost of sales. The other accounts are either less directly involved (accounts receivable and inventories) or not involved in the ratio (dividends, travel and entertainment).

2. **(C)** The current ratio is equal to current assets / current liabilities. Both accounts payable and the line of credit increased significantly during the year and are in the denominator of the equation—thus resulting in a decrease in the ratio. Increases in current assets inventory and accounts receivable, by themselves, would increase, not decrease, the ratio. Utilities and insurance are accounts not directly reflected in the ratio. A decrease in accounts receivable is incorrect because, in this situation, accounts receivable increased. Likewise, an increase in the allowance for doubtful accounts did not occur.

3. **(F)** The quick ratio is equal to quick assets (here cash and accounts receivable) divided by current liabilities. The over $3,000,000 increase in accounts payable had a much greater effect on the ratio than did the approximately $20,000 decrease in cash or the $6,520 amortization of leasehold improvements. Likewise, even if the $28,000 decrease in capital lease obligations—noncurrent went into a current liability account the effect is much smaller than that of accounts payable.

4. **(A)** The risk increases as the average receivable is older than in the past (on top of this, something is seriously wrong with bad debt expense as apparently nothing was added to it this year). The decrease in the turnover has no necessary tie to future sales or to the completeness of this year's accounts receivable. If anything, the lower turnover would represent the opposite, year 5 sales recorded in year 4 sales and accounts receivables. There is no indication here of consignments (which should not be included in accounts receivable until the goods are sold).

5. **(B)** Because there were no changes in the account (other than the amortization), none of the listed procedures is appropriate.

6. **(C)** Cash receipts received after year-end will in general identify accounts that have been collected and for which no allowance is ordinarily required. While cash collections reduce receivables prior to year-end (either shortly before year-end, from throughout the year or those related party transactions), they do not provide significant evidence with respect to those unpaid as of year-end.

7. **(D)** As described, these costs do not seem capitalizable as software development costs; they should be recorded as general research and development expense until their technological feasibility has been established (FASB ASC 985-20-25-1). The other replies all suggest that these are capitalizable costs.

Analytical Procedures

Task-Based Simulation 3

aicpa.tbs.analytical.proc.001_18

Research		
	Authoritative Literature	
		Help

Copyright ©2018 by the American Institute of Certified Public Accountants, Inc., is reprinted and/or adapted with permission.

The auditors of STA, Inc., a calendar-year corporation, obtained the selected information for Years 1 and 2 located in the exhibit above.

The auditors are performing analytical procedures relative to the expectations of expenses for Year 2 and have established a materiality threshold of 5% of the auditors' expected Year 2 amount.

For each of the expenses in column A, consider the additional notes in column B and complete the following:

- In column C, enter the auditors' expectations of Year 2 expense.
- In column D, select the auditors' decision as to whether further testing is needed and why.
- Round all amounts to the nearest dollar.
- An option may be used once, more than once, or not at all.
- Consider each account independently.

A	B	C	D		
		Auditors' expectation	**Auditors' decision**		
Expenses	**Additional notes**		**(A)**	**(B)**	**(C)**
1. Salary	Average salaries increased 2% effective January 1, Year 2. Average headcount was 200 in Year 1 and 300 in year 2. A. Above acceptable amount, further testing needed B. Below acceptable amount, further testing needed C. Within threshold, no further testing needed		○	○	○

(Continued)

A	B	C	D		
		Auditors' expectation	Auditors' decision		
Expenses	Additional notes		(A)	(B)	(C)
2. Rent	**Building 1:** On July 1, Year 2, the company entered into a new lease agreement. Monthly rent expense was 5% higher than that of the prior lease. **Building 2:** The company began renting another facility on January 1, Year 2, for $45,000 a month, on a month-to-month basis. A. Above acceptable amount, further testing needed B. Below acceptable amount, further testing needed C. Within threshold, no further testing needed		○	○	○
3. Utilities	The utilities expense is based on square footage of each facility; the rate did not change from Year 1 to Year 2. A. Above acceptable amount, further testing needed B. Below acceptable amount, further testing needed C. Within threshold, no further testing needed		○	○	○
4. Miscellaneous	Calculation is based on 0.25% gross revenue. A. Above acceptable amount, further testing needed B. Below acceptable amount, further testing needed C. Within threshold, no further testing needed		○	○	○
5. Repairs and maintenance	Repairs and maintenance expense is based on the average gross value of assets at cost January 1, Year 1: $2,700,000 January 1, Year 2: $3,300,000 January 1, Year 3: $3,700,000 A. Above acceptable amount, further testing needed B. Below acceptable amount, further testing needed C. Within threshold, no further testing needed		○	○	○
6. Interest expense	The average interest rate of STA's debt is 7%. A. Above acceptable amount, further testing needed B. Below acceptable amount, further testing needed C. Within threshold, no further testing needed		○	○	○

Exhibit Title: 01 Financial Information

Financial Information

The auditors of STA, Inc. obtained the following selected account information:

Selected information	Year 2	Year 1
Gross revenue	$63,000,000	$60,000,000
Net income before taxes	11,650,000	11,000,000
Salary expense	12,500,000	8,000,000
Rent expense	1,920,000	1,200,000
Utilities expense	155,000	120,000
Depreciation expense	705,000	675,000
Repairs and maintenance	375,000	300,000
Interest expense	523,000	338,100
Miscellaneous	151,000	135,000
Tax expense	4,325,150	3,850,000

Additionally, the auditors noted the following information:
- STA rents space in an office building:
  - Space in Building 1: 25,000 sq. ft.
- On January 1, year 2, the company added a second space:
  - Space in Building 2: 11,000 sq. ft.
- The balance of interest-bearing debt outstanding:
  - January 1, year 2: $4,830,000
  - December 31, year 2: $10,262,000
  - The company issued additional debt on July 1, year 2

Answers and Explanations

Task-Based Simulation 3 Solution

Research			
	Authoritative Literature		
		Help	

A	B	C	D		
		Auditors' expectation	**Auditors' decision**		
Expenses	**Additional notes**		**(A)**	**(B)**	**(C)**
1. Salary	Average salaries increased 2% effective January 1, Year 2. Average headcount was 200 in Year 1 and 300 in year 2. A. Above acceptable amount, further testing needed B. Below acceptable amount, further testing needed C. Within threshold, no further testing needed	12,240,000	○	○	●
2. Rent	Building 1: On July 1, Year 2, the company entered into a new lease agreement. Monthly rent expense was 5% higher than that of the prior lease. Building 2: The company began renting another facility on January 1, Year 2, for $45,000 a month, on a month-to-month basis. A. Above acceptable amount, further testing needed B. Below acceptable amount, further testing needed C. Within threshold, no further testing needed	1,770,000	●	○	○
3. Utilities	The utilities expense is based on square footage of each facility; the rate did not change from Year 1 to Year 2. A. Above acceptable amount, further testing needed B. Below acceptable amount, further testing needed C. Within threshold, no further testing needed	172,800	○	●	○

A	B	C	D		
		Auditors' expectation	Auditors' decision		
Expenses	Additional notes		(A)	(B)	(C)
4. Miscellaneous	Calculation is based on 0.25% gross revenue. A. Above acceptable amount, further testing needed B. Below acceptable amount, further testing needed C. Within threshold, no further testing needed	157,500	○	○	●
5. Repairs and maintenance	Repairs and maintenance expense is based on the average gross value of assets at cost January 1, Year 1: $2,700,000 January 1, Year 2: $3,300,000 January 1, Year 3: $3,700,000 A. Above acceptable amount, further testing needed B. Below acceptable amount, further testing needed C. Within threshold, no further testing needed	350,000	●	○	○
6. Interest expense	The average interest rate of STA's debt is 7%. A. Above acceptable amount, further testing needed B. Below acceptable amount, further testing needed C. Within threshold, no further testing needed	528,200	○	○	●

Salary Expense:

Year 1: Average salary = $8,000,000/200 employees = $40,000/Employee

In Year 2, the company had 300 employees and increased salaries by 2%.

Year 2 expectation: $40,000/Employee × 300 employees × 1.02 = **$12,240,000**

Materiality = 5% × Expectation → $12,240,000 × .05 = **$612,000**

Difference = Actual expense – Expectation → $12,500,000 – $12,240,000 = **$260,000**

Since the difference is within the materiality threshold, no further testing is required.

Rent Expense:

In Year 2, building #1 was unchanged for the first half of the year, but for the second half of the year rent increased by 5%. In addition, the company added building #2 in the second half of the year.

Year 2 expectation:

Building #1: ($1,200,000 × 6/12) + ($1,200,000 × 6/12 × 1.05) =	**$1,230,000**
Building #2: $45,000/Month × 12 months =	**540,000**
	$1,770,000

Materiality = 5% × Expectation → $1,770,000 × .05 = **$88,500**

Difference = Actual expense − Expectation → $1,920,000 − $1,770,000 = **$150,000**

Since the difference is above the acceptable amount (by more than the materiality threshold), further testing is required.

Utilities Expense:

Utilities are based on the square footage of the building(s), and the rate did not change in Year 2.

Year 2 Expectation:

Year 1 rate:	$120,000/25,000 sq. ft. =	$4.80/sq. ft.
Building #1:	25,000 sq. ft. × $4.80/sq. ft. =	$120,000
Building #2:	11,000 sq. ft. × $4.80/sq. ft. =	52,800
	Total	**$172,800**

Materiality = 5% × Expectation → $172.800 × .05 = **$8640**

Difference = Actual expense − Expectation → $155,000 − $172,800 = **($17,800)**

Since the difference is below the acceptable amount (by more than the materiality threshold), further testing is required.

Miscellaneous Expense:

This is calculated as .25% of gross revenue.

Year 2 Expectation = .25% × $63,000,000 =	**$157,500**
Materiality = 5% × Expectation → $157,500 × .05 =	**$7875**
Difference = Actual expense − Expectation → $151,000 − $157,500 =	**($6500)**

Since the difference is within the materiality threshold, no further testing is required.

Repairs & Maintenance Expense:

This is based on average gross cost of assets, the cost of which is given for Year 1, Year 2, and Year 3 as of January 1.

Year 2 expectation:

Year 1 average gross cost:	($2,700,000 + $3,300,000)/2 = $3,000,000
Year 2 average gross cost:	($3,300,000 + $3,700,000)/2 = $3,500,000
Percentage increase in gross cost:	$3,500,000/$3,000,000 = 7/6
Year 2 expectation = Year 1 expense × 7/6 = $300,000 × 7/6 =	**$350,000**

Materiality = 5% × Expectation → $350,000 = **$17,500**

Difference = Actual expense − Expectation → $375,000 − $350,000 = **$25,000**

Since the difference is above the acceptable amount (by more than the materiality threshold), further testing is required.

Interest Expense:

Year 2 Expectation:

Jan. 1–June 30, Year 2:	$4,830,000 × .07 × 6/12 =	$169,050
July 1–Dec. 31, Year 2:	$10,262,000 × .07 × 6/12 =	$359,170
Total		**$528,220**

Materiality = 5% × Expectation → $528,220 = **$26,411**

Difference = Actual expense − Expectation → $523,000 − $528,220 = **($5220)**

Since the difference is within the materiality threshold, no further testing is required.

Performing Further Procedures and Obtaining Evidence

Audit Evidence: Concepts and Standards

Assertions and Types of Audit Procedures

Task-Based Simulation 4

aicpa.tbs.gen.is.evidence2.001_08

Effects on Audit Risk Components		
	Authoritative Literature	
		Help

Copyright ©2008 by the American Institute of Certified Public Accountants, Inc., is reprinted and/or adapted with permission.

Based on knowledge of the company and its environment, including its internal control, auditors have assessed the risk of material misstatements in the client's financial statements, whether due to error or fraud, and designed the nature, timing, and extent of further audit procedures to be performed during the audit engagement. The company has a calendar year-end and operates only on weekdays.

As a result of conducting these risk assessment procedures, the audit program for Year 2 includes several changes from the audit program for Year 1.

In conducting Year 2 audit procedures for unrecorded liabilities, the materiality/scope for this area was assessed by the auditors at $6,000. Adjustments are only recorded for items equal to or exceeding materiality.

The last day of field work is estimated to be February 1, Year 3.

For the items reflected in the following check register, which are not recorded in the accounts payable subsidiary ledger as of December 31, Year 2, determine if each potential liability is recorded in the proper accounting period and also determine the amount that should be journalized, if any. If no action is required, you must enter $0.

Client's Check Register

Vendor	Check#	Check Date	Amount	Nature of the expenses
Water World Distributors, Inc.	1333	1/6/Year 3	$3,500	Water coolers for office and warehouse delivered 12/31/Year 2
Daniel Breen, Esquire	1334	1/6/Year 3	$6,000	Corporate legal services for December, Year 2
Telephone Services, Inc.	1335	1/8/Year 3	$6,500	December, Year 2 telephone and computer services
Payroll processing—Paychecks	1336	1/10/Year 3	$25,500	Bi-weekly payroll—pay period 12/25/Year 2 through 1/7/Year 3
Pitt Ohio Trucking Company	1337	1/10/Year 3	$45,601	Trucking services 12/4/Year 2 through 1/3/Year 3; deliveries were made evenly throughout the period
Petty cash	1338	1/17/Year 3	$2,002	Replenish petty cash box
Smith's Forklift Repairs	1339	1/22/Year 3	$11,000	Received new fork lift on 12/29/Year 2; ordered unit on 12/18/Year 2
Glenn's Glass Distribution Center	1340	1/23/Year 3	$12,230	Specialty goods ordered 12/20/Year 2 and delivered 12/31/Year 2
Payroll processing—Paychecks	1341	1/24/Year 3	$25,500	Bi-weekly payroll—pay period 1/8/Year 3 through 1/15/Year 3
Daniel Breen, Esquire	1342	2/6/Year 3	$6,800	Corporate legal services for January, Year 3

For each of the check numbers in the table below, click on each of the associated cells and select from the two lists provided whether any action or adjustment is required or not, as well as the dollar value of the required adjustment. Each selection may be used once, more than once, or not at all.

Adjustment needed?	Amount
A. No action required	A. $0
B. Adjustment	B. $2,002
	C. $2,970
	D. $3,500
	E. $4,413
	F. $6,000
	G. $6,500
	H. $6,800
	I. $7,650
	J. $9,900
	K. $11,000
	L. $12,230
	M. $12,750
	N. $25,500
	O. $41,188
	P. $45,601

Check #	Adjustment needed? (A)	(B)	Amount (A)	(B)	(C)	(D)	(E)	(F)	(G)	(H)	(I)	(J)	(K)	(L)	(M)	(N)	(O)	(P)
1333	○	○	○	○	○	○	○	○	○	○	○	○	○	○	○	○	○	○
1334	○	○	○	○	○	○	○	○	○	○	○	○	○	○	○	○	○	○
1335	○	○	○	○	○	○	○	○	○	○	○	○	○	○	○	○	○	○
1336	○	○	○	○	○	○	○	○	○	○	○	○	○	○	○	○	○	○
1337	○	○	○	○	○	○	○	○	○	○	○	○	○	○	○	○	○	○
1338	○	○	○	○	○	○	○	○	○	○	○	○	○	○	○	○	○	○
1339	○	○	○	○	○	○	○	○	○	○	○	○	○	○	○	○	○	○
1340	○	○	○	○	○	○	○	○	○	○	○	○	○	○	○	○	○	○
1341	○	○	○	○	○	○	○	○	○	○	○	○	○	○	○	○	○	○
1342	○	○	○	○	○	○	○	○	○	○	○	○	○	○	○	○	○	○

Answers and Explanations

Task-Based Simulation 4 Solution

Effects on Audit Risk Components		
	Authoritative **Literature**	
		Help

Check #	Adjustment needed? (A)	(B)	Amount (A)	(B)	(C)	(D)	(E)	(F)	(G)	(H)	(I)	(J)	(K)	(L)	(M)	(N)	(O)	(P)
1333	●	○	●	○	○	○	○	○	○	○	○	○	○	○	○	○	○	○
1334	○	●	○	○	○	○	○	●	○	○	○	○	○	○	○	○	○	○
1335	○	●	○	○	○	○	○	○	●	○	○	○	○	○	○	○	○	○
1336	○	●	○	○	○	○	○	○	○	○	○	○	○	○	●	○	○	○
1337	○	●	○	○	○	○	○	○	○	○	○	○	○	○	○	○	●	○
1338	●	○	●	○	○	○	○	○	○	○	○	○	○	○	○	○	○	○
1339	○	●	○	○	○	○	○	○	○	○	○	○	●	○	○	○	○	○
1340	○	●	○	○	○	○	○	○	○	○	○	○	○	●	○	○	○	○
1341	●	○	●	○	○	○	○	○	○	○	○	○	○	○	○	○	○	○
1342	●	○	●	○	○	○	○	○	○	○	○	○	○	○	○	○	○	○

Rationale

(A, A) Check #1333 was written to Water World Distributors, Inc. for water coolers that were delivered on December 31. The amount of the check, $3,500, falls under the materiality limit of $6,000 so no action is required. The amount to be entered is 0.

(B, F) Check #1334 was written to Daniel Breen, Esquire, for legal services rendered in December. The amount of the check, $6,000, is equal to the materiality limit. An adjusting journal entry is needed for $6,000.

(B, G) Check #1335 was written to Telephone Services, Inc. for phone services rendered in December. The check amount, $6,500, exceeds the materiality limit of $6,000. An adjusting journal entry is needed for $6,500.

(B, M) Check #1336 was written to Payroll Processing for the weekly payroll that extended from 12/25 to 1/7, a two week period with 10 working days. Half of the $25,500 payroll needs to be accrued as of 12/31. An adjusting entry is needed for $12,750.

(B, O) Check #1337 was written to Pitt Ohio Trucking Company for trucking services from 12/4 through 1/3. This is a 31-day period with the deliveries specified as having been made evenly throughout the period. 28 out of the 31 days or 28/31 of the check amount of $45,601 needs to be accrued as of 12/31. An adjusting journal entry is needed for $41,188.

(A, A) Check #1338 was written to Petty Cash to replenish the petty cash box. The amount of the check, $2,002, falls below the materiality limit of $6,000. No action is needed and the amount is 0.

(B, K) Check #1339 was written to Smith's Forklift Repairs for a new forklift that was received on 12/29. The amount of the check, $11,000, exceeds the materiality limit of $6,000. An adjusting entry for $11,000 is needed.

(B, L) Check #1340 was written to Glenn's Glass Distribution Center for goods that were delivered on 12/31. The amount of the check, $12,230, exceeds the materiality limit of $6,000. An adjusting journal entry is needed for $12,230.

(A, A) Check #1341 was written to Payroll Processing for a January payroll period. As the services were rendered in January, no action is needed and the amount is 0.

(A, A) Check #1342 was written to Daniel Breen, Esquire, for legal services rendered in January. This is an expense of the new year, Year 3. No action is required and the amount is 0.

Forming Conclusions and Reporting

Audit Reports

Audits of Group Financial Statements

Task-Based Simulation 5

TBSAWB0097

Research

    Authoritative Literature

        Help

You have been assigned to the audit of the Kieso Company, a nonissuer of securities to the public. Suppose that your firm will issue an unmodified audit report on Kieso Company's financial statements for fiscal years ended December 31, 20X1 and 20X2. A wholly-owned subsidiary, Weygandt Company, was audited by other auditors. The other auditors, Horngren & Associates, issued their unmodified audit report on Weygandt's financial statements for fiscal years ending December 31, 20X1 and 20X2 on March 15, 20X3.

Locate the paragraph which identifies the restrictions that exist on an auditor's ability to make reference to component auditors when issuing an audit report on group financial statements.

Choose a title from the list.

Select a title from the dropdown list below.

AU-C	§		·	

ℹ Some examples of correctly formatted AU responses are AU§123.45, AU§123.A567

Answer

Research

    Authoritative Literature

        Help

Type the paragraph here.

Correctly formatted AU-C paragraphs start with an optional upper case letter, followed by 1, 2 or 3 digits.

AU-C	§	600	·	25

ℹ Some examples of correctly formatted AU responses are AU§123.45, AU§123.A567
